NINJA FOODI SMARTLID

COOKBOOK

for Beginners UK

1800 Super Easy Ninja Foodi Smartlid Recipes to Make Any Family Flavor | Incl. Pressure Cook, Air Fry, Grill, Bake, Steam and More

Delisa A. Gordon

CONTENTS

4   INTRODUCTION

8   BREAKFAST

20   SNACKS, APPETIZERS & SIDES

32   SOUPS & STEWS

43   VEGAN & VEGETABLE

55   POULTRY

67   BEEF, PORK & LAMB

80   FISH & SEAFOOD

93   DESSERTS

105   APPENDIX A : MEASUREMENT CONVERSIONS

107   APPENDIX B : RECIPES INDEX

INTRODUCTION

Meet Delisa A. Gordon, a culinary enthusiast with a flair for simplifying cooking using cutting-edge kitchen tech. Her passion for innovative cooking methods has led her to create a cookbook that promises to revolutionize your kitchen experience. With a background in culinary arts and a dedication to making meals more efficient and delightful, Delisa is your trusted guide in exploring the endless possibilities of the Ninja Foodi SmartLid.

In today's fast-paced world, where convenience is key, the Ninja Foodi SmartLid emerges as a culinary game-changer. Delisa A. Gordon's Ninja Foodi SmartLid Cookbook unlocks the potential of this revolutionary kitchen appliance, offering a gateway to simpler, more delicious cooking. Whether you're a seasoned chef or a kitchen novice, this cookbook is your secret ingredient to crafting gourmet meals, comfort food classics, and healthy dishes with ease.

Inside these pages, you'll discover a treasure trove of recipes to suit all tastes and dietary preferences. Delisa's recipes are designed to elevate your culinary skills and transform your meals. But this cookbook is more than just recipes; it's a culinary masterclass. Delisa shares her expertise, simplifying complex cooking techniques and providing valuable tips to make the most of your Ninja Foodi SmartLid.

Delisa's Ninja Foodi SmartLid Cookbook is your invitation to a culinary adventure filled with creativity, flavor, and convenience. It's your key to becoming a kitchen virtuoso, effortlessly mastering the art of cooking with this innovative appliance. Whether you're a busy professional, a home cook looking for efficiency, or an adventurous food lover, this cookbook is your trusted companion.

Get ready to be inspired, save time in the kitchen, and relish every bite of your homemade creations. Experience the future of cooking with Delisa A. Gordon, where delicious meals are just a lid away.

The Ninja Foodi SmartLid is a game-changing kitchen innovation designed to simplify your cooking experience. This high-tech lid is compatible with Ninja Foodi appliances and is equipped with advanced sensors and automation capabilities. It intelligently detects the type of food you're cooking and automatically adjusts cooking time and temperature to ensure your dishes turn out perfectly every time. With the Ninja Foodi SmartLid, you can say goodbye to the guesswork in the kitchen and enjoy consistently delicious meals with minimal effort. Its user-friendly digital display makes it accessible to cooks of all levels, making it a must-have tool for anyone looking to elevate their culinary skills and save time in the kitchen.

COOKING MODES OF NINJA FOODI SMARTLID

Pressure Cooking: Ideal for quickly cooking ingredients while retaining flavor and moisture.

Slow Cooking: Perfect for creating tender, slow-cooked dishes with rich flavors.

Sear/Sauté: Allows you to brown and sear ingredients directly in the SmartLid before pressure cooking.

Steam: Steam vegetables, seafood, and more to preserve nutrients and taste.

Bake/Roast: Achieve crispy, golden results when baking or roasting your favorite dishes.

Broil: Quickly brown the tops of casseroles, melt cheese, or add a finishing touch.

Dehydrate: Preserve fruits, vegetables, and meats by removing moisture for long-lasting snacks.

Keep Warm: Maintain your dishes at the perfect serving temperature until you're ready to eat.

Ingredient	Cooking Mode	Temperature (°F)	Cooking Time (Minutes)
Chicken (Breasts)	Pressure Cook	165°F	10-15
Beef (Stew)	Slow Cook or Sear	250-300°F	4-8 hours or 20-30
Rice	Pressure Cook or Steam	212-240°F	6-15
Vegetables	Steam	190-212°F	5-10
Salmon	Bake	350-400°F	10-15
Pork (Pulled)	Slow Cook or Sear	250-300°F	6-8 hours or 20-30
Desserts (Cake)	Bake	325-375°F	30-45

7 REASONS FOR NINJA FOODI SMARTLID COOKBOOK

MAXIMIZE YOUR NINJA FOODI SMARTLID

This cookbook is your key to unlocking the full potential of your Ninja Foodi SmartLid. It provides comprehensive guidance on how to use and make the most of this versatile kitchen appliance attachment.

STREAMLINE COOKING PROCESSES

With the cookbook's recipes and instructions, you can streamline your cooking processes. It offers time-saving techniques and tips, making meal preparation more efficient, especially for busy individuals and families.

DIVERSE AND DELICIOUS RECIPES

You'll find a wide range of recipes in this cookbook, from quick weeknight dinners to gourmet dishes. The diverse selection ensures that there's something to satisfy every palate, and it introduces you to new flavors and cuisines.

HEALTHY EATING MADE EASY

For those looking to maintain a healthier lifestyle, this cookbook has you covered. It features recipes that focus on nutrition without compromising on taste, helping you make better food choices.

BOOST YOUR CULINARY SKILLS

Whether you're a novice or an experienced cook, the cookbook provides valuable cooking tips and techniques. It helps you enhance your culinary skills, empowering you to tackle more complex recipes with confidence.

INSPIRATION FOR EVERY OCCASION

No matter the occasion, the cookbook offers recipe ideas. Whether you're planning a casual family meal, a special celebration, or just want to try something new, you'll find inspiration within its pages.

SAVES YOU MONEY

Dining out can be costly, but with this cookbook, you can create restaurant-quality meals at home. It's a budget-friendly way to enjoy delicious dishes without the expense of eating out.

Breakfast

Homemade Vanilla Yogurt.9
Spinach Casserole..............9
Hearty Breakfast Muffins ..9
Cheesy Shakshuka............10
Deviled Eggs 10
Cinnamon Apple Bread 10
Sausage & Egg Stuffed
Peppers 11
Ham & Broccoli Frittata...11
Banana Custard Oatmeal ..11
Peaches & Brown Sugar
Oatmeal 12
Savory Custards With Ham
And Cheese.......................12
Cheesy Meat Omelet 12
Cinnamon Roll Monkey
Bread 13
Chocolate Chip And Banana
Bread Bundt Cake 13
Vanilla Banana Bread 13
Bell Pepper Frittata...........14

Butternut Squash Cake
Oatmeal 14
Breakfast Egg Pizza..........14
Chorizo Omelet 15
Flaxseeds Granola 15
Pumpkin Breakfast Bread.15
Cranberry Lemon Quinoa.16
Walnut Orange Coffee Cake
16
Poached Egg Heirloom
Tomato..............................16
Brussels Sprouts Bacon Hash
17
Pancetta Hash With Baked
Eggs 17
Apple Walnut Quinoa.......17
Prosciutto Egg Bake 18
Baked Eggs & Kale 18
Sweet Bread Pudding 18
Double Berry Dutch Baby 19
Baked Eggs In Spinach.....19

Homemade Vanilla Yogurt

Servings:6
Cooking Time: 8 Hours

Ingredients:
- ½ gallon whole milk
- 3 tablespoons plain yogurt with active live cultures
- ½ tablespoon vanilla extract
- ½ cup honey

Directions:
1. Pour the milk into the pot. Assemble pressure lid, making sure the pressure release valve is in the VENT position.
2. Select YOGURT and set time to 8 hours. Select START/STOP to begin.
3. After the milk has boiled, the display will read COOL.
4. Once cooled, the unit will beep and display ADD & STIR. Remove pressure lid. Add the plain yogurt and whisk until fully incorporated. Reassemble pressure lid, making sure the pressure release valve is still in the VENT position.
5. When incubating is complete after 8 hours, transfer the yogurt to a glass container or bowl, cover, and refrigerate for a minimum of 8 hours.
6. Once the yogurt has chilled, stir in the vanilla and honey until well combined. Cover and place the glass bowl back in the refrigerator or divide the yogurt into airtight glass jars. The yogurt may be refrigerated up to 2 weeks.

Nutrition Info:
- Calories: 286,Total Fat: 11g,Sodium: 133mg,Carbohydrates: 38g,Protein: 11g.

Spinach Casserole

Servings: 4
Cooking Time: 5 Minutes

Ingredients:
- 4 whole eggs
- 1 tablespoons milk
- 1 tomato, diced
- ½ cup spinach
- ¼ teaspoon salt
- ¼ teaspoon black pepper

Directions:
1. Take a baking pan small enough to fit Ninja Foodi and grease it with butter.
2. Take a medium bowl and whisk in eggs, milk, salt, pepper, add veggies to the bowl and stir.
3. Pour egg mixture into the baking pan and lower the pan into the Ninja Foodi .
4. Close Air Crisping lid and Air Crisp for 325 degrees for 7 minutes.
5. Remove the pan from eggs, and enjoy hot.

Nutrition Info:
- Calories: 78; Fat: 5g; Carbohydrates: 1 g; Protein: 7 g

Hearty Breakfast Muffins

Servings: 12
Cooking Time: 20 Minutes

Ingredients:
- ½ cup brown sugar
- 3 eggs
- 1/3 cup coconut oil, melted
- 1/3 cup applesauce, unsweetened
- ¼ cup orange juice
- 1 tsp vanilla
- 2 cups whole wheat flour
- 2 tsp baking soda
- 2 tsp cinnamon
- ¼ tsp salt
- 1 ½ cup carrots, grated
- 1 cup apple, grated
- ¼ cup pecans, chopped

Directions:
1. Set to bake function on 375°F. Line 2 6-cup muffin tins with paper liners.
2. In a large bowl, whisk together sugar, eggs, oil, applesauce, orange juice, and vanilla.
3. Stir in flour, baking soda, cinnamon, and salt just until combined.
4. Fold in carrots, apple, and pecans and mix well. Divide evenly among prepared muffin tins.
5. Place tins, one at a time, in the cooker and add the tender-crisp lid. Bake 20-25 minutes, or until muffins

pass the toothpick test. Repeat.

6. Let cool in pan 10 minutes, then transfer to wire rack to cool completely.

Nutrition Info:

• Calories 206,Total Fat 9g,Total Carbs 28g,Protein 5g,Sodium 288mg.

Cheesy Shakshuka

Servings: 4
Cooking Time: 50 Min

Ingredients:

• 1 small red onion; chopped
• 2 cans diced tomatoes with their juice /435ml
• ½ red bell pepper, seeded and chopped
• 1 medium banana pepper, seeded and minced
• 4 eggs
• ⅓ cup crumbled goat cheese /84g
• 2 garlic cloves; chopped
• 2 tbsp fresh cilantro; chopped /30g
• 3 tbsps ghee /45g
• ½ tsp smoked paprika /7.5g
• ½ tsp red chili flakes /2.5g
• ¼ tsp black pepper; freshly ground /1.25g
• 1 tsp salt /5g
• ½ tsp coriander, ground /2.5g

Directions:

1. Choose Sear/Sauté on you Foodi and set on Medium to preheat the inner pot; press Start. Melt the ghee and sauté the onion, bell pepper, banana pepper, and garlic. Season lightly with salt and cook for 2 minutes until the vegetables are fragrant and beginning to soften.

2. Then, stir in the tomatoes, coriander, smoked paprika, red chili flakes, and black pepper. Seal the pressure lid, choose pressure and adjust the pressure to High and the timer to 4 minutes. Press Start to continue cooking.

3. When the timer has read to the end, perform a quick pressure release. Gently crack the eggs onto the tomato sauce in different areas. Seal the pressure lid again, but with the valve set to Vent. Choose Steam and adjust the cook time to 3 minutes. Press Start to cook the eggs.

4. When ready, carefully open the pressure lid. Sprinkle with the shakshuka with goat cheese and cilantro. Dish into a serving platter and serve.

Deviled Eggs

Servings: 4
Cooking Time: 10 Minutes

Ingredients:

• 8 large eggs
• 1 cup of water
• Guacamole
• Sliced Radishes
• Mayonnaise
• Furikake

Directions:

1. Add water to the inner insert of your Ninja Foodi.

2. Place the steamer rack inside the pot and set the eggs on top of the rack.

3. Lock pressure lid and cook on "HIGH" pressure for 6 minutes.

4. Release Pressure naturally over 10 minutes and transfer the eggs to a suitable full of icy water.

5. Peel after 5 minutes.

6. Cut in half and decorate with guacamole, sliced radish, mayo and enjoy.

Nutrition Info:

• Calories: 70; Fat: 6g; Carbohydrates: 1g; Protein: 3g

Cinnamon Apple Bread

Servings: 10
Cooking Time: 55 Minutes

Ingredients:

• Butter flavored cooking spray
• ½ cup coconut flour
• 1 ½ cup almond flour, sifted
• ¾ cup Stevia
• 1 tsp baking soda
• 2 tbsp. cinnamon
• 5 eggs
• 1 cup applesauce, unsweetened

Directions:

1. Set to bake function on 350°F. Lightly spray a loaf pan with cooking spray.

2. In a large bowl, combine both flours, Stevia, cinnamon, and baking soda.

3. In a medium bowl, whisk the eggs and applesauce together. Add to dry ingredients and stir to combine.

4. Pour into prepared pan and place in the cooker. Add the tender-crisp lid and bake 45-55 minutes, or until bread passes the toothpick test.

5. Let cool 15 minutes, then invert onto serving plate

and slice.

Nutrition Info:
• Calories 189, Total Fat 10g, Total Carbs 30g, Protein 7g, Sodium 162mg.

Sausage & Egg Stuffed Peppers

Servings: 4
Cooking Time: 6 Hours

Ingredients:
• ½ lb. breakfast sausage
• 4 bell peppers
• ½ cup water
• 6 eggs
• ½ cup cheddar Jack cheese, grated
• 4 oz. green chilies, diced
• ¼ tsp salt
• 1/8 tsp pepper
• 2 tbsp. green onion, diced

Directions:
1. Set cooker to sauté on med-high heat.
2. Add sausage and cook, breaking up with spatula, until no longer pink. Transfer to a bowl and drain off the grease.
3. Cut the tops off the peppers and remove the seeds and ribs. Place in the cooking pot and pour the water around them.
4. In a medium bowl, whisk eggs until smooth. Stir in cheese, chilies, salt, and pepper until combined. Fill the peppers with the egg mixture.
5. Secure the lid and set to slow cooker function on high. Set the timer for 4 hours.
6. Casserole is done when the eggs are set, if not done when the timer goes off, cook another 1-2 hours. Garnish with green onions and serve.

Nutrition Info:
• Calories 364, Total Fat 22g, Total Carbs 15g, Protein 27g, Sodium 874mg.

Ham & Broccoli Frittata

Servings: 6
Cooking Time: 30 Minutes

Ingredients:
• 1 tbsp. butter, soft
• 1 cup red pepper, seeded & sliced
• 1 cup ham, cubed
• 2 cups broccoli florets
• 4 eggs

• 1 cup half-n- half
• 1 cup cheddar cheese, grated
• 1 tsp salt
• 2 tsp pepper
• 2 cups water

Directions:
1. Use the soft butter to grease a 6x3-inch baking dish.
2. Place the peppers in an even layer on the bottom of the dish. Top with ham then broccoli.
3. In a mixing bowl, whisk together eggs, half-n-half, salt, and pepper.
4. Stir in cheese and pour mixture over ingredients in the baking dish. Cover with foil.
5. Pour 2 cups water into the cooking pot and place the rack inside.
6. Place the baking dish on the rack and secure the lid. Select pressure cooking on high and set the timer for 20 minutes.
7. When the timer goes off, release pressure naturally for 10 minutes, then quick release.
8. Remove the baking dish and let cool at least 5 minutes. With a sharp knife, loosen the sides of the frittata then invert onto serving plate. Serve immediately.

Nutrition Info:
• Calories 401, Total Fat 29g, Total Carbs 9g, Protein 26g, Sodium 1487mg.

Banana Custard Oatmeal

Servings: 6
Cooking Time: 40 Minutes

Ingredients:
• Butter flavored cooking spray
• 1 2/3 cups vanilla almond milk, unsweetened
• 2 large bananas, mashed
• 1 cup bananas, sliced
• 1 cup steel cut oats
• 1/3 cup maple syrup
• 1/3 cup walnuts, chopped
• 2 eggs, beaten
• 1 tbsp. butter, melted
• 1 ½ tsp cinnamon
• 1 tsp baking powder
• 1 tsp vanilla extract
• ½ tsp nutmeg
• ¼ teaspoon salt
• 2 ½ cups water

Directions:
1. Spray a 1 1/2 –quart baking dish with cooking

spray.

2. In a large bowl, combine all ingredients thoroughly. Transfer to prepared baking dish.

3. Pour 1 ½ cups water into the cooking pot and add the trivet. Place dish on the trivet and secure the lid.

4. Select pressure cooking on high and set timer for 40 minutes.

5. When timer goes off, release pressure naturally for 10 minutes, then use quick release. Stir oatmeal well then serve.

Nutrition Info:
• Calories 349,Total Fat 10g,Total Carbs 56g,Protein 10g,Sodium 281mg.

Peaches & Brown Sugar Oatmeal

Servings: 8
Cooking Time: 8 Hours

Ingredients:
• Nonstick cooking spray
• 2 cups steel cut oats
• 8 cups water
• 1 tsp cinnamon
• ½ cup brown sugar
• 1 tsp vanilla
• 1 cup peaches, cubed

Directions:
1. Spray cooking pot with cooking spray.
2. Add the oats, water, cinnamon, sugar, and vanilla to the pot, stir to combine.
3. Secure the lid and select slow cooker function on low. Set timer for 8 hours.
4. Stir in peaches and serve.

Nutrition Info:
• Calories 231,Total Fat 3g,Total Carbs 46g,Protein 7g,Sodium 7mg.

Savory Custards With Ham And Cheese

Servings: 4
Cooking Time: 40 Min

Ingredients:
• 4 large eggs
• 1 ounce cottage cheese; at room temperature /30g
• 2 serrano ham slices; halved widthwise
• ¼ cup caramelized white onions /32.5g
• ¼ cup half and half /62.5ml
• ¼ cup grated Emmental cheese /32.5g
• ¼ tsp salt /1.25g
• Ground black pepper to taste

Directions:
1. Preheat the inner pot by choosing Sear/Sauté and adjust to Medium; press Start. Put the serrano ham in the pot and cook for 3 to 4 minutes or until browned, turning occasionally.

2. Remove the ham onto a paper towel-lined plate. Next, use a brush to coat the inside of four 1- cup ramekins with the ham fat. Set the cups aside, then, empty and wipe out the inner pot with a paper towel, and return the pot to the base.

3. Crack the eggs into a bowl and add the cottage cheese, half and half, salt, and several grinds of black pepper. Use a hand mixer to whisk the Ingredients until co cheese lumps remain.

4. Stir in the grated emmental cheese and mix again to incorporate the cheese. Lay a piece of ham in the bottom of each custard cup. Evenly share the onions among the cups as well as the egg mixture. Cover each cup with aluminum foil.

5. Pour 1 cup or 250ml of water into the inner pot and fix the reversible rack in the pot. Arrange the ramekins on top. Lock the pressure lid in Seal position; choose Pressure, adjust to High, and set the timer to 7 minutes. Press Start.

6. After cooking, perform a quick pressure release. Use tongs to remove the custard cups from the pressure cooker. Cool for 1 to 2 minutes before serving.

Cheesy Meat Omelet

Servings: 2
Cooking Time: 20 Min

Ingredients:
• 1 beef sausage; chopped
• 4 slices prosciutto; chopped
• 1 cup grated mozzarella cheese /130g
• 4 eggs
• 3 oz. salami; chopped /90g
• 1 tbsp chopped onion /15g
• 1 tbsp ketchup /15ml

Directions:
1. Preheat the Ninja Foodi to 350 °F or 177°C on Air Crisp mode. Whisk the eggs with the ketchup, in a bowl. Stir in the onion. Spritz the inside of the Ninja Foodi basket with a cooking spray. Add and brown the sausage for about 2 minutes.

2. Meanwhile, combine the egg mixture, mozzarella cheese, salami and prosciutto. Pour the egg mixture over the sausage and stir it. Close the crisping lid and cook for 10 minutes. Once the timer beeps, ensure the omelet is just set. Serve immediately.

Cinnamon Roll Monkey Bread

Servings:8
Cooking Time: 20 Minutes

Ingredients:
- 4 eggs
- ¼ cup whole milk
- 1 teaspoon vanilla extract
- ½ teaspoon cinnamon
- Cooking spray
- 2 tubes refrigerated cinnamon rolls with icing, quartered

Directions:
1. In a medium bowl, whisk together the eggs, milk, vanilla, and cinnamon.
2. Lightly coat the pot with cooking spray, then place the cinnamon roll pieces in the pot. Pour the egg mixture over the dough. Close crisping lid.
3. Select BAKE/ROAST, set temperature to 350°F, and set time to 20 minutes. Select START/STOP to begin.
4. When cooking is complete, remove pot from unit and place it on a heat-resistant surface. Remove lid. Let cool for 5 minutes, then top with the icing from the cinnamon rolls and serve.

Nutrition Info:
- Calories: 327,Total Fat: 12g,Sodium: 710mg,Carbohydrates: 46g,Protein: 7g.

Chocolate Chip And Banana Bread Bundt Cake

Servings:8
Cooking Time: 40 Minutes

Ingredients:
- 2 cups all-purpose flour
- 1 teaspoon baking soda
- ¼ teaspoon cinnamon
- ¼ teaspoon sea salt
- 1 stick (½ cup) unsalted butter, at room temperature
- ½ cup dark brown sugar
- ¼ cup granulated sugar
- 2 eggs, beaten

- 1 teaspoon vanilla extract
- 3 ripe bananas, mashed
- 1 cup semisweet chocolate chips
- Cooking spray

Directions:
1. Close crisping lid. Select BAKE/ROAST, set temperature to 325°F, and set time to 5 minutes. Select START/STOP to begin preheating.
2. In a medium bowl, stir together the flour, baking soda, cinnamon, and salt.
3. In a large bowl, beat together the butter, brown sugar, and granulated sugar. Stir in the eggs, vanilla, and bananas.
4. Slowly add the dry mixture to wet mixture, stirring until just combined. Fold in chocolate chips.
5. Use cooking spray to grease the Ninja Tube Pan or a 7-inch Bundt pan. Pour the batter into the pan.
6. Once preheated, place pan on the Reversible Rack in the lower position. Close crisping lid.
7. Select BAKE/ROAST, set temperature to 325°F, and set time to 40 minutes. Select START/STOP to begin.
8. After 30 minutes, open lid and check doneness by inserting a toothpick into the cake. If it comes out clean, it is done. If not, continue baking until done.
9. When cooking is complete, remove pan from pot and place on a cooling rack for 30 minutes before serving.

Nutrition Info:
- Calories: 484,Total Fat: 21g,Sodium: 238mg,Carbohydrates: 70g,Protein: 6g.

Vanilla Banana Bread

Servings: 8
Cooking Time: 50 Minutes

Ingredients:
- 2 cups flour
- 1 teaspoon baking powder
- ½ cup erythritol
- ½ cup butter softened
- 2 eggs
- 1 tablespoon vanilla extract
- 4 bananas, peeled and mashed

Directions:
1. Grease a 7-inch springform pan.
2. In a suitable, mix flour and baking powder.
3. In another bowl, add erythritol, butter, and eggs and beat until creamy.

4. Add the bananas and vanilla extract and beat until well combined.
5. Slowly add flour mixture, 1 cup at a time, and mix until smooth.
6. Place mixture into prepared loaf pan evenly.
7. In the Ninja Foodi's insert, place 1 cup of water.
8. Set the "Reversible Rack" in the Ninja Foodi's insert.
9. Place the pan over the "Reversible Rack."
10. Close the Ninja Foodi's lid with the pressure lid and place the pressure valve to the "Seal" position.
11. Select "Pressure" mode and set it to "High" for 50 minutes.
12. Press the "Start/Stop" button to initiate cooking.
13. Switch the pressure valve to "Vent" and do a "Quick" release.
14. Cut into desired sized slices and serve.

Nutrition Info:
• Calories: 336; Fat: 13.1 g; Carbohydrates: 50.4 g; Protein: 5.4g

Bell Pepper Frittata

Servings: 2
Cooking Time: 18 Minutes

Ingredients:
• 1 tablespoon olive oil
• 1 chorizo sausage, sliced
• 1½ cups bell peppers, seeded and chopped
• 4 large eggs
• Black pepper and salt, as required
• 2 tablespoons feta cheese, crumbled
• 1 tablespoon fresh parsley, chopped

Directions:
1. Select the "Sauté/Sear" setting of Ninja Foodi and place the butter into the pot.
2. Press the "Start/Stop" button to initiate cooking and heat for about 2-3 minutes.
3. Add the sausage and bell peppers and cook for 6-8 minutes or until golden brown.
4. Meanwhile, in a suitable bowl, add the eggs, salt, and black pepper and beat well.
5. Press the "Start/Stop" button to pasue cooking and place the eggs over the sausage mixture, followed by the cheese and parsley.
6. Close the Ninja Foodi's lid with a crisping lid and select "Air Crisp."
7. Set its cooking temperature to 355 °F for 10 minutes.

8. Press the "Start/Stop" button to initiate cooking.
9. Open the Ninja Foodi's lid and transfer the frittata onto a platter.
10. Cut into equal-sized wedges and serve hot.

Nutrition Info:
• Calories: 398; Fat: 31g; Carbohydrates: 8g; Protein: 22.9g

Butternut Squash Cake Oatmeal

Servings: 4
Cooking Time: 35 Min

Ingredients:
• 1 cup steel-cut oats /130g
• ⅓ cup honey /84ml
• 3 ½ cups coconut milk /875ml
• ¼ cup toasted walnuts; chopped /32.5g
• 1 cup shredded Butternut Squash /250ml
• ½ cup sultanas /65g
• ¼ tsp ground nutmeg /1.25g
• 1 tsp ground cinnamon /5g
• ½ tsp vanilla extract /2.5ml
• ½ tsp fresh orange zest /2.5g
• ¾ tsp ground ginger /3.75g
• ½ tsp salt /2.5g
• ½ tsp sugar /2.5g

Directions:
1. In the pressure cooker, mix sultanas, orange zest, ginger, milk, honey, squash, salt, oats, and nutmeg.
2. Seal the pressure lid, choose Pressure, set to High, and set the timer to 12 minutes; press Start. When ready, do a natural pressure release for 10 minutes. Into the oatmeal, stir in the vanilla extract and sugar. Top with walnuts and serve.

Breakfast Egg Pizza

Servings: 8
Cooking Time: 28 Minutes

Ingredients:
• 12 eggs
• 1/2 cup heavy cream
• 1/2 tsp salt
• 1/4 tsp pepper
• 8 oz sausage
• 2 cups peppers sliced
• 1 cup cheese shredded

Directions:
1. Heat peppers in a bowl for 3 minutes in the micro-

wave.

2. Place air crisper basket in the Ninja Foodi and place the bacon in it.

3. Secure the Ninja Foodi lid and Air Fry them for 10 minutes.

4. Transfer the cooked crispy bacon to a plate and keep them aside.

5. Whisk eggs with salt, pepper, and cream in a bowl.

6. Pour this mixture in a greased baking pan.

7. Place the trivet in the Ninja Food cooking pot and set the baking pan over it.

8. Secure the Ninja Foodi lid and turn the pressure valve to 'closed' position.

9. Select 'Bake/Roast' for 15 minutes at 350 °F.

10. Once done, top the egg bake with cheese and peppers.

11. Broil this pizza for 3 minutes in the broiler until the cheese melts.

12. Serve warm.

Nutrition Info:

- Calories 489; Total Fat 43.3g; Total Carbs 5g; Protein 22.2 g

Chorizo Omelet

Servings: 4
Cooking Time: 30-35 Minutes

Ingredients:

- 3 eggs, whisked
- 3 ounces chorizo, chopped
- 1-ounces Feta cheese, crumbled
- 5 tablespoons almond milk
- ¾ teaspoon chilli flakes
- ¼ teaspoon salt
- 1 green pepper, chopped

Directions:

1. Add listed ingredients to a suitable and mix well.

2. Take an omelette pan and pour the mixture on it.

3. Pre-heat your Ninja Food on "BAKE" mode at a temperature of 320 °F.

4. Transfer pan with omelette mix to your Ninja Foodi and cook for 30 minutes, or until the surface is golden and the egg has set properly.

5. Serve and enjoy.

Nutrition Info:

- Calories: 426; Fat: 38g; Carbohydrates: 7g; Protein: 21g

Flaxseeds Granola

Servings: 16
Cooking Time: 2½ Hours

Ingredients:

- ½ cup sunflower kernels
- 5 cups mixed nuts, crushed
- 2 tablespoons ground flax seeds
- ¼ cup olive oil
- ½ cup unsalted butter
- 1 teaspoon ground cinnamon
- 1 cup choc zero maple syrup

Directions:

1. Grease the Ninja Foodi's insert.

2. In the greased Ninja Foodi's insert, add sunflower kernels, nuts, flax seeds, oil, butter, and cinnamon and stir to combine.

3. Close the Ninja Foodi's lid with a crisping lid and select "Slow Cooker."

4. Set on "High" for 2½ hours.

5. Press the "Start/Stop" button to initiate cooking.

6. Stir the mixture after every 30 minutes.

7. Open the Ninja Foodi's lid and transfer the granola onto a large baking sheet.

8. Add the maple syrup and stir to combine.

9. Set aside to cool completely before serving.

10. You can preserve this granola in an airtight container.

Nutrition Info:

- Calories: 189; Fat: 10 g; Carbohydrates: 7.7 g; Protein: 4.6 g

Pumpkin Breakfast Bread

Servings: 14
Cooking Time: 3 Hours

Ingredients:

- Nonstick cooking spray
- 2 cups whole wheat pastry flour
- 1 ½ tsp baking soda
- 2 tsp pumpkin pie spice
- ½ cup coconut oil, melted
- ¾ cup honey
- 2 eggs
- 3 cups pumpkin puree
- 1 tsp. vanilla extract
- 1 banana, mashed
- ½ cup walnuts, chopped & divided

Directions:

1. Spray the cooking pot with cooking spray.
2. In a large bowl, combine flour, baking soda, and pumpkin spice.
3. Make a "well" in the middle of the dry ingredients and add oil, honey, eggs, pumpkin, vanilla, and banana, and ¼ cup of the walnuts. Mix well to thoroughly combine all ingredients.
4. Pour batter into cooking pot and sprinkle remaining walnuts over the top. Place two paper towels over the top of the pot and secure the lid. Select slow cooking function on high. Set timer for 2 hours.
5. When timer goes off check bread, it should pass the toothpick test. If it is not done, continue cooking another 30-60 minutes.
6. When bread is done, transfer to a wire rack to cool.

Nutrition Info:
• Calories 207,Total Fat 9g,Total Carbs 30g,Protein 4g,Sodium 130mg.

Cranberry Lemon Quinoa

Servings: 6
Cooking Time: 20 Minutes

Ingredients:
• 16 oz. quinoa
• 4 ½ cups water
• ½ cup brown sugar, packed
• 1 tsp lemon extract
• ½ tsp salt
• ½ cup cranberries, dried

Directions:
1. Add all ingredients, except the cranberries, to the cooker and stir to mix.
2. Secure the lid and select pressure cooking on high. Set timer for 20 minutes.
3. When timer goes off, use natural release for 10 minutes. Then use quick release and remove the lid.
4. Stir in cranberries and serve.

Nutrition Info:
• Calories 284,Total Fat 4g,Total Carbs 56g,Protein 8g,Sodium 152mg.

Walnut Orange Coffee Cake

Servings: 8
Cooking Time: 25 Minutes

Ingredients:
• Butter flavor cooking spray
• 1 cup Stevia
• 1/4 cup butter, unsalted, soft
• 1 egg
• 2 tsp orange zest, grated
• ½ tsp vanilla
• 1/8 tsp cinnamon
• 2 cups whole wheat flour
• 1 tsp baking soda
• ½ cup orange juice, fresh squeezed
• ½ cup water
• ½ cup walnuts, chopped

Directions:
1. Select bake function and heat cooker to 350°F. Spray a 7-inch round pan with cooking spray.
2. In a medium bowl, beat Stevia and butter until smooth.
3. Add egg, zest, vanilla, and cinnamon and mix until combined.
4. In a separate bowl, combine dry ingredients. Add to butter mixture and mix until thoroughly combined. Stir in nuts.
5. Spread batter in prepared pan and place in the cooker. Secure the tender-crisp lid and bakke 20-25 minutes, or until it passes the toothpick test.
6. Let cool in pan 10 minutes, then invert onto wire rack. Serve warm.

Nutrition Info:
• Calories 203,Total Fat 10g,Total Carbs 53g,Protein 6g,Sodium 170mg.

Poached Egg Heirloom Tomato

Servings: 4
Cooking Time: 10 Min

Ingredients:
• 4 large eggs
• 2 large Heirloom ripe tomatoes; halved crosswise
• 4 small slices feta cheese
• 1 cup water /250ml
• 2 tbsp grated Parmesan cheese /30g
• 1 tsp chopped fresh herbs, of your choice /5g
• Salt and black pepper to taste
• Cooking spray

Directions:
1. Pour the water into the Ninja Foodi and fit the reversible rack. Grease the ramekins with the cooking spray and crack each egg into them.
2. Season with salt and pepper. Cover the ramekins with aluminum foil. Place the cups on the trivet. Seal the lid.

3. Select Steam mode for 3 minutes on High pressure. Press Start/Stop.Once the timer goes off, do a quick pressure release. Use a napkin to remove the ramekins onto a flat surface.

4. In serving plates, share the halved tomatoes, feta slices, and toss the eggs in the ramekin over on each tomato half. Sprinkle with salt and pepper, parmesan, and garnish with chopped herbs.

Brussels Sprouts Bacon Hash

Servings: 4
Cooking Time: 20 Minutes

Ingredients:
- 1/2 lb. brussels sprouts, sliced in half
- 4 slices bacon, chopped
- 1/2 red onion, chopped
- salt, to taste
- black pepper, to taste

Directions:
1. Toss all the ingredients into the Ninja Foodi cooking pot.
2. Secure the Ninja Foodi lid and turn its pressure handle to 'Closed' position.
3. Select mode for 20 minutes at 390 °F.
4. Once done, release the steam naturally then remove the lid.
5. Serve fresh.

Nutrition Info:
- Calories 121; Total Fat 9 g; Total Carbs 13.8 g; Protein 4.3 g

Pancetta Hash With Baked Eggs

Servings: 4
Cooking Time: 50 Min

Ingredients:
- 6 slices pancetta; chopped
- 2 potatoes, peeled and diced
- 4 eggs
- 1 white onion; diced
- 1 tsp freshly ground black pepper /5g
- 1 tsp garlic powder /5g
- 1 tsp sweet paprika /5g
- 1 tsp salt /5g

Directions:
1. Choose Sear/Sauté, set to Medium High, and choose Start/Stop to preheat the pot for 5 minutes.
2. Once heated, lay the pancetta in the pot, and cook, stirring occasionally; for 5 minutes, or until the pancetta is crispy.
3. Stir in the onion, potatoes, sweet paprika, salt, black pepper, and garlic powder. Close the crisping lid; choose Bake/Roast, set the temperature to 350°F or 177°C, and the time to 25 minutes. Cook until the turnips are soft and golden brown while stirring occasionally.
4. Crack the eggs on top of the hash, close the crisping lid, and choose Bake/Roast. Set the temperature to 350°F or 177°C, and the time to 10 minutes.
5. Cook the eggs and check two or three times until your desired crispiness has been achieved. Serve immediately.

Apple Walnut Quinoa

Servings: 2
Cooking Time: 15 Minutes

Ingredients:
- ½ cup quinoa, rinsed
- 1 apple, cored & chopped
- 2 cups water
- ½ cup apple juice, unsweetened
- 2 tsp maple syrup
- 1 tsp cinnamon
- ¼ cup walnuts, chopped & lightly toasted

Directions:
1. Set the cooker to sauté on med-low heat. Add the quinoa and apples and cook, stirring frequently, 5 minutes.
2. Add water and apple juice and stir to mix. Secure the lid and set to pressure cooking on high. Set timer for 10 minutes.
3. When timer goes off use quick release to remove the lid. Quinoa should be tender and the liquid should be absorbed, if not cook another 5 minutes.
4. When quinoa is done, stir in syrup and cinnamon. Sprinkle nuts over top and serve.

Nutrition Info:
- Calories 348,Total Fat 12g,Total Carbs 54g,Protein 9g,Sodium 7mg.

Prosciutto Egg Bake

Servings: 4
Cooking Time: 45 Min

Ingredients:
- 8 ounces prosciutto; chopped /240g
- 1 cup shredded Monterey Jack cheese /130g
- 1 cup water /250ml
- 1 cup whole milk /250ml
- 1 orange bell pepper, seeded and chopped
- 4 eggs
- 1 tsp salt /5g
- 1 tsp freshly ground black pepper /5g

Directions:
1. Break the eggs into a bowl, pour in the milk, salt, and black pepper and whisk until combined. Stir in the Monterey Jack Cheese.
2. Put the bell pepper and prosciutto in the cake pan. Then, pour over the egg mixture, cover the pan with aluminum foil and put on the reversible rack.
3. Put the rack in the pot and pour in the water. Seal the pressure lid, choose pressure and set to High. Set the time to 20 minutes and choose Start/Stop.
4. When done cooking, do a quick pressure release and carefully remove the lid that is after the pressure has completely escaped.
5. When baking is complete, take the pan out of the pot and set it on a heatproof surface, and cool for 5 minutes.

Baked Eggs & Kale

Servings: 4
Cooking Time: 25 Minutes

Ingredients:
- 1 tbsp. olive oil
- 6 cups kale, remove stems & chop
- 2 cloves garlic, diced fine
- ¼ cup ricotta cheese, fat free
- ¼ cup feta, fat free, crumbled
- 4 eggs
- 1/3 cup grape tomatoes, halved
- ¼ tsp pepper
- ½ tsp salt

Directions:
1. Add oil to the cooking pot and select sauté on medium heat.
2. Add the kale and garlic and cook until kale is wilted, about 2-3 minutes.
3. In a small bowl, combine ricotta and feta cheeses.
4. Make 4 small indents in the kale mixture and crack an egg into each one.
5. Drop the cheese mixture by tablespoons around the eggs.
6. Top with tomatoes, pepper, and salt. Secure the tender-crisp lid, set to air fryer function at 350°F and bake 20-25 minutes or until egg whites are cooked through. Serve immediately.

Nutrition Info:
- Calories 154, Total Fat 12g, Total Carbs 7g, Protein 7g, Sodium 410mg.

Sweet Bread Pudding

Servings: 3
Cooking Time: 45 Min

Ingredients:
- 8 slices of bread
- 2 eggs
- ¼ cup sugar /32.5g
- ¼ cup honey /62.5ml
- 1 cup milk /250ml
- ½ cup buttermilk /125ml
- 4 tbsp raisins /60g
- 2 tbsp chopped hazelnuts /30g
- 2 tbsp butter, softened /30g
- ½ tsp vanilla extract /2.5ml
- Cinnamon for garnish

Directions:
1. Beat the eggs along with the buttermilk, honey, milk, vanilla, sugar, and butter. Stir in raisins and hazelnuts. Cut the bread into cubes and place it in a bowl.
2. Pour the milk mixture over the bread. Let soak for about 10 minutes. Close the crisping lid and cook the bread pudding for 25 minutes on Roast mode. Leave the dessert to cool for 5 minutes, then invert onto a plate and sprinkle with cinnamon to serve.

Double Berry Dutch Baby

Servings: 6
Cooking Time: 25 Minutes

Ingredients:
- 1 tbsp. butter, melted
- 2 eggs
- ½ cup skim milk
- 1 tsp vanilla
- ½ cup flour
- ¼ tsp cinnamon
- 1/8 tsp salt
- 2 tbsp. sugar
- 2 tsp cornstarch
- 1/3 cup water
- ½ cup strawberries, sliced
- ½ cup blueberries

Directions:
1. Select air fryer function and heat cooker to 400°F. Pour melted butter in an 8-inch round pan and swirl to coat bottom.
2. In a medium bowl, whisk together eggs, milk, and vanilla.
3. In a small bowl, combine flour, cinnamon, and salt. Whisk into egg mixture until smooth. Pour into prepared pan.
4. Place in the cooker and secure the tender-crisp lid. Bake 18-20 minutes until golden brown and set in the center.
5. Remove pancake from the cooker and set to sauté on medium heat.
6. Add sugar, cornstarch, and water to the cooking pot and stir until smooth.
7. Stir in both berries and bring to a boil. Cook about 5 minutes, stirring frequently, until berries have softened and mixture has thickened. Spoon into pancake, slice and serve.

Nutrition Info:
- Calories 125,Total Fat 4g,Total Carbs 17g,Protein 4g,Sodium 100mg.

Baked Eggs In Spinach

Servings: 4
Cooking Time: 20 Minutes

Ingredients:
- 2 tsp olive oil
- 2 cloves garlic, diced fine
- 4 cups baby spinach
- ½ cup parmesan cheese, reduced fat
- 4 eggs
- 1 tomato, diced fine

Directions:
1. Select sauté function on medium heat. Add oil to the pot and heat.
2. Add the spinach and garlic and cook, stirring, about 2 minutes, or until spinach has wilted. Drain off excess liquid.
3. Stir in parmesan cheese. Make 4 small indents in the spinach. Crack an egg into each indent.
4. Set to air fryer function at 350°F. Secure the tender-crisp lid and bake 15-20 minutes or until egg whites are cooked and yolks are still slightly runny.
5. Let cool 5 minutes, serve topped with tomatoes.

Nutrition Info:
- Calories 139,Total Fat 10g,Total Carbs 3g,Protein 12g,Sodium 280mg.

Snacks, Appetizers & Sides

Chicken Bites 21
Artichoke Bites.................21
South Of The Border Corn Dip 22
Apple Pecan Cookie Bars.22
Salmon Croquettes 22
Gingered Butternut Squash22
Crispy Cheesy Zucchini Bites.................................23
Herb Roasted Mixed Nuts 23
Butter-flower Medley 23
Sweet Potato Gratin..........24
Asian Chicken Nuggets 24
Cheesy Tomato Bruschetta25
Crab Rangoon's 25
Mexican Street Corn Queso Dip 25
Crispy Chicken Skin.........26
Strawberry Snack Bars 26

Steak And Minty Cheese ..26
Pistachio Stuffed Mushrooms 27
Crispy Delicata Squash 27
Mini Crab Cakes...............27
Potato Samosas.................28
Glazed Walnuts.................28
Scalloped Potatoes............28
Crispy Onion Rings 29
Tangy Jicama Chips..........29
Spicy Black Bean Dip 29
Green Bean Casserole 30
Herby Fish Skewers..........30
Cumin Baby Carrots 30
Cheesy Onion Dip 31
Zesty Brussels Sprouts With Raisins 31
Sweet Potato Fries 31

Chicken Bites

Servings:4
Cooking Time: 8 Minutes

Ingredients:
- ½ cup Italian seasoned bread crumbs
- 2 tablespoons grated Parmesan cheese
- ¼ teaspoon sea salt
- ¼ teaspoon freshly ground black pepper
- 1 boneless, skinless chicken breast, cut into 1-inch pieces
- ½ cup unsalted butter, melted
- Cooking spray

Directions:
1. Place Cook & Crisp Basket in pot. Close crisping lid. Select AIR CRISP, set temperature to 390°F, and set time to 5 minutes. Select START/STOP to begin preheating.
2. In a medium bowl, combine the bread crumbs, Parmesan cheese, salt, and pepper. In a separate medium bowl, toss the chicken in the butter until well coated. Move a few of the chicken pieces to the breadcrumb mixture and coat. Repeat until all the chicken is coated.
3. Once unit is preheated, open lid and place the chicken bites in the basket in a single layer. Coat well with cooking spray. Close lid.
4. Select AIR CRISP, set temperature to 390°F, and set time to 8 minutes. Select START/STOP to begin.
5. After 4 minutes, open lid, then lift basket and flip the chicken bites with silicone-tipped tongs. Coat well with cooking spray. Lower basket back into pot and close lid to continue cooking.
6. After 4 minutes, check for desired crispness. Cooking is complete when the internal temperature of the chicken reads at least 165°F on a food thermometer.

Nutrition Info:
- Calories: 279,Total Fat: 25g,Sodium: 246mg,Carbohydrates: 5g,Protein: 10g.

Artichoke Bites

Servings: 8
Cooking Time: 70 Min

Ingredients:
- ¼ cup frozen chopped kale /32.5g
- ¼ cup finely chopped artichoke hearts /32.5g
- ¼ cup goat cheese /32.5g
- ¼ cup ricotta cheese /32.5g
- 4 sheets frozen phyllo dough, thawed
- 1 lemon, zested
- 1 large egg white
- 1 tbsp olive oil /15ml
- 2 tbsps grated Parmesan cheese /30ml
- 1 tsp dried basil /5g
- ½ tsp salt /2.5g
- ½ tsp freshly ground black pepper /2.5g

Directions:
1. In a bowl, mix the kale, artichoke hearts, ricotta cheese, parmesan cheese, goat cheese, egg white, basil, lemon zest, salt, and pepper. Put the Crisping Basket in the pot. Close the crisping lid, choose Air Crisp, set the temperature to 375°F or 191°C, and the time to 5 minutes; press Start/Stop.
2. Then, place a phyllo sheet on a clean flat surface. Brush with olive oil, place a second phyllo sheet on the first, and brush with oil. Continue layering to form a pile of four oiled sheets.
3. Working from the short side, cut the phyllo sheets into 8 strips. Cut the strips in half to form 16 strips.
4. Spoon 1 tbsp of filling onto one short side of every strip. Fold a corner to cover the filling to make a triangle; continue repeatedly folding to the end of the strip, creating a triangle-shaped phyllo packet. Repeat the process with the other phyllo bites.
5. Open the crisping lid and place half of the pastry in the basket in a single layer. Close the lid, Choose Air Crisp, set the temperature to 350°F or 177°C, and the timer to 12 minutes; press Start/Stop.
6. After 6 minutes, open the lid, and flip the bites. Return the basket to the pot and close the lid to continue baking. When ready, take out the bites into a plate. Serve warm.

South Of The Border Corn Dip

Servings: 8
Cooking Time: 2 Hours

Ingredients:
- 33 oz. corn with chilies
- 10 oz. tomatoes & green chilies, diced
- 8 oz. cream cheese, cubed
- ½ cup cheddar cheese, grated
- ¼ cup green onions, chopped
- ½ tsp garlic, diced fine
- ½ tsp chili powder

Directions:
1. Place all ingredients in the cooking pot and stir to mix.
2. Add the lid and set to slow cooking function on low heat. Set timer for 2 hours. Stir occasionally.
3. Dip is done when all the cheese is melted and it's bubbly. Stir well, then transfer to serving bowl and serve warm.

Nutrition Info:
- Calories 225, Total Fat 13g, Total Carbs 24g, Protein 7g, Sodium 710mg.

Apple Pecan Cookie Bars

Servings: 12
Cooking Time: 20 Minutes

Ingredients:
- Nonstick cooking spray
- 2/3 cup sugar
- 2 egg whites
- ½ tsp vanilla
- ½ cup flour
- 1 tsp baking powder
- 2 cups Granny Smith apples, chopped
- ¼ cup pecans, chopped

Directions:
1. Lightly spray an 8-inch baking pan with cooking spray.
2. In a large bowl, whisk together egg whites, sugar, and vanilla until frothy.
3. Whisk in flour and baking powder until combined.
4. Fold in apples and nuts and pour into pan.
5. Place the rack in the cooking pot and place the pan on it. Add the tender-crisp lid and set to air fry on 350°F. Bake 18-20 minutes or until the cookies pass the toothpick test.
6. Let cool before cutting and serving.

Nutrition Info:
- Calories 90, Total Fat 2g, Total Carbs 18g, Protein 1g, Sodium 10mg.

Salmon Croquettes

Servings: 6
Cooking Time: 20 Minutes

Ingredients:
- Nonstick cooking spray
- 14 ¾ oz. pink salmon, drained, bones removed & flaked
- 1 egg
- 2 tbsp. yellow mustard
- 2 tsp fresh parsley, chopped
- ½ tsp onion powder
- ¼ tsp pepper
- ¾ cup herb-seasoned stuffing mix
- ½ cup flour

Directions:
1. Lightly spray fryer basket with cooking spray.
2. In a large bowl, combine salmon, egg, mustard, parsley, onion powder, and pepper and mix well. Form into 12 patties.
3. Place the flour in a shallow dish.
4. Dredge both sides of the patties in the flour and place in the basket in a single layer.
5. Add the tender-crisp lid and set to air fry on 375°F. Cook patties 8-10 minutes per side until gold brown. Serve immediately.

Nutrition Info:
- Calories 245, Total Fat 7g, Total Carbs 24g, Protein 19g, Sodium 670mg.

Gingered Butternut Squash

Servings: 6
Cooking Time: 15 Minutes

Ingredients:
- 8 cups butternut squash, peeled, seeded, & cut in 1-inch cubes
- 1 cup water
- ½ tsp salt
- 4 tbsp. butter
- ¼ cup half n half
- 3 tbsp. honey
- ½ tsp ginger
- ¼ tsp cinnamon

Directions:

1. Add the squash, water, and salt to the cooking pot, stir.

2. Add the lid and select pressure cooking on high. Set timer for 12 minutes. When the timer goes off, use quick release to remove the lid.

3. Drain the squash and place in a large bowl.

4. Add remaining ingredients. Set cooker to saute on medium heat. Cook until butter melts, stirring occasionally

5. Once the butter melts, pour the sauce over the squash and mash with a potato masher. Serve.

Nutrition Info:
- Calories 198,Total Fat 9g,Total Carbs 31g,Protein 2g,Sodium 267mg.

Crispy Cheesy Zucchini Bites

Servings: 6
Cooking Time: 10 Minutes

Ingredients:
- 2 zucchini, cut in 3/4-inch thick slices
- Nonstick cooking spray
- ½ cup panko bread crumbs
- 1 tbsp. parmesan cheese
- 1 tbsp. lite mayonnaise
- ½ tsp garlic powder
- ½ tsp onion powder
- ¼ tsp seasoned salt
- ¼ tsp pepper

Directions:
1. Pour enough water to cover the bottom of the cooking pot about 1 inch. Set to sauté on high heat and bring to a boil.

2. Add zucchini, reduce heat to low and simmer 3-5 minutes or just until tender. Drain and pat dry with paper towels.

3. Lightly spray the fryer basket with cooking spray and place it in the cooking pot.

4. In a small bowl, stir together bread crumbs, cheese, garlic powder, onion powder, salt, and pepper.

5. Spread one side of each zucchini slice with mayonnaise and place in a single layer in the basket. Sprinkle crumb mixture over top of each slice.

6. Add tender-crisp lid and set to air fry on 450°F. Bake 3-5 minutes, or until golden brown. Serve immediately.

Nutrition Info:
- Calories 48,Total Fat 1g,Total Carbs 7g,Protein 1g,Sodium 196mg.

Herb Roasted Mixed Nuts

Servings: 12
Cooking Time: 15 Minutes

Ingredients:
- ½ cup pecan halves
- ½ cup raw cashews
- ½ cup walnut halves
- ½ cup hazelnuts
- ½ cup Brazil nuts
- ½ cup raw almonds
- 1 tbsp. fresh rosemary, chopped
- 1 tbsp. fresh thyme, chopped
- ½ tbsp. fresh parsley, chopped
- 1 tsp garlic granules
- ½ tsp paprika
- ½ tsp salt
- ¼ tsp pepper
- ½ tbsp. olive oil

Directions:
1. Combine all ingredients in a large bowl and toss to coat thoroughly.

2. Pour the nuts in the fryer basket and place in the cooking pot. Add the tender-crisp lid and select air fry on 375°F. Cook 10 minutes, then stir the nuts around.

3. Cook another 5-10 minutes, stirring every few minutes and checking to make sure they don't burn. Serve warm.

Nutrition Info:
- Calories 229,Total Fat 21g,Total Carbs 7g,Protein 5g,Sodium 99mg.

Butter-flower Medley

Servings: 10
Cooking Time: 15 Minutes

Ingredients:
- 3 cups butternut squash, peel & cut in 1-inch cubes
- 1 head cauliflower, separated into florets
- 2 cloves garlic
- 1 tbsp. skim milk
- ½ tsp onion powder
- ¼ tsp thyme
- 1/8 tsp salt
- 1/8 tsp black pepper
- 1 tbsp. butter
- 1 tbsp. parmesan cheese, reduced fat

Directions:
1. Add the squash, cauliflower, and garlic to the cook-

ing pot. Pour in ½ cup water. Add the lid and select pressure cooking on high. Set the timer for 8 minutes.

2. When timer goes off use natural release to remove the lid. Drain the vegetables and place in a large bowl.

3. Add remaining ingredients, except parmesan, and beat until smooth.

4. Transfer the squash mixture back to the cooking pot and sprinkle top with parmesan cheese. Add the tender-crisp lid and select air fry on 400°F. Cook 5-6 minutes or until top is lightly browned. Serve.

Nutrition Info:
• Calories 47,Total Fat 1g,Total Carbs 8g,Protein 2g,-Sodium 68mg.

Sweet Potato Gratin

Servings:6
Cooking Time: 15 Minutes

Ingredients:
• 2 tablespoons unsalted butter
• 3 tablespoons all-purpose flour
• 2 cups heavy (whipping) cream, warmed in microwave
• 2 teaspoons kosher salt
• 1 teaspoon pumpkin pie spice
• ¼ cup water
• 3 large sweet potatoes, peeled and cut in half, then cut into half-moons ¼-inch thick
• 1¼ cups shredded Cheddar cheese, divided
• ½ cup chopped walnuts or pecans, or slivered almonds

Directions:
1. Select SEAR/SAUTÉ and set to MD:HI. Select START/STOP to begin. Let preheat for 5 minutes.

2. Add the butter. Once melted, add the flour and stir together until a thick paste forms, about 1 minute. (The combination of butter and flour is called a roux). Continue cooking the roux for 2 minutes, stirring frequently with a rubber-coated whisk. Slowly add the warm cream while continuously whisking so there are no lumps, about 3 minutes. The cream should be thickened.

3. Add the salt and pumpkin pie spice and whisk to incorporate. Whisk in the water and let the mixture simmer for 3 minutes.

4. Place the potatoes in the pot. Assemble pressure lid, making sure the pressure release valve is in the SEAL position.

5. Select PRESSURE and set to LO. Set time to 1

minute. Select START/STOP to begin.

6. When pressure cooking is complete, quick release pressure by moving the pressure release valve to the VENT position. Carefully remove lid when unit has finished releasing pressure.

7. Add ¼ cup of cheese and stir gently to incorporate, being careful not to break up the cooked potatoes. Ensure mixture is flat, then cover top with remaining 1 cup of cheese. Sprinkle the nuts over the cheese. Close crisping lid.

8. Select BROIL and set time to 5 minutes. Select START/STOP to begin.

9. When cooking is complete, open lid and let the gratin cool for 10 minutes before serving.

Nutrition Info:
• Calories: 536,Total Fat: 47g,Sodium: 409mg,Carbohydrates: 20g,Protein: 10g.

Asian Chicken Nuggets

Servings: X
Cooking Time: 20 Minutes

Ingredients:
• 1 lb. chicken breasts, boneless, skinless & cut in 1-inch pieces
• 1 tsp salt
• ½ tsp pepper
• 2 eggs
• 1 cup Panko bread crumbs
• ¼ cup lite soy sauce
• ¼ cup honey
• 4 cloves garlic, diced fine
• 2 tbsp. hoisin sauce
• 1 tablespoon freshly grated ginger
• 1 tablespoon Sriracha
• 2 green onions, sliced thin
• 2 tsp sesame seeds

Directions:
1. Place the rack in the cooking pot and top with a sheet of parchment paper.

2. Sprinkle the chicken with salt and pepper.

3. In a shallow dish, beat the eggs.

4. Place the bread crumbs in a separate shallow dish. Working in batches, dip the chicken first in the eggs then bread crumbs, pressing to coat the chicken well.

5. Place the chicken on the parchment paper in a single layer. Add the tender-crisp lid and select air fry on 400 °F. Bake the chicken 10-15 minutes until golden brown and cooked through, turning over halfway

through cooking time. Transfer to serving plate and keep warm.

6. Set the cooker to sauté on med-high heat. Add the soy sauce, honey, garlic, hoisin, ginger, and Sriracha, stir to combine. Cook, stirring frequently, until sauce thickens, about 2 minutes.

7. Add chicken and toss to coat. Serve immediately garnished with green onions and sesame seeds.

Nutrition Info:
• Calories 304,Total Fat 7g,Total Carbs 27g,Protein 32g,Sodium 1149mg.

Cheesy Tomato Bruschetta

Servings: 2
Cooking Time: 15 Min

Ingredients:
• 1 Italian Ciabatta Sandwich Bread
• 2 tomatoes; chopped
• 2 garlic cloves, minced
• 1 cup grated mozzarella cheese /130g
• Olive oil to brush
• Basil leaves; chopped
• Salt and pepper to taste

Directions:
1. Cut the bread in half, lengthways, then each piece again in half. Drizzle each bit with olive oil and sprinkle with garlic. Top with the grated cheese, salt, and pepper.

2. Place the bruschetta pieces into the Ninja Foodi basket, close the crisping lid and cook for 12 minutes on Air Crisp mode at 380 °F or 194°C. At 6 minutes, check for doneness.

3. Once the Ninja Foodi beeps, remove the bruschetta to a serving platter, spoon over the tomatoes and chopped basil to serve.

Crab Rangoon's

Servings: 15
Cooking Time: 20 Minutes

Ingredients:
• Nonstick cooking spray
• 8 oz. cream cheese, reduced fat, soft
• 1 tsp garlic powder
• 2 cups crab meat, chopped
• ¼ cup green onion, sliced thin
• 30 wonton wrappers

Directions:

1. Lightly spray the fryer basket with cooking spray.
2. In a medium bowl, beat cream cheese and garlic powder until smooth.
3. Stir in crab and onions and mix well.
4. Spoon a teaspoon of crab mixture in the center of each wrapper. Lightly brush edges with water and fold in half. Press edges to seal and lay in a single layer of the basket.
5. Add the tender-crisp lid and set to air fry on 350°F. Bake 15-20 minutes until crisp and golden brown, turning over halfway through cooking time. Serve immediately.

Nutrition Info:
• Calories 236,Total Fat 3g,Total Carbs 15g,Protein 11g,Sodium 416mg.

Mexican Street Corn Queso Dip

Servings:8
Cooking Time: 20 Minutes

Ingredients:
• 1 package cream cheese, quartered
• 6 ounces cotija cheese, crumbled, 2 ounces reserved for topping
• 1 can fire-roasted tomatoes with chiles
• ½ cup mayonnaise
• Zest of 2 limes
• Juice of 2 limes
• 2 packages shredded Mexican cheese blend, divided
• 1 garlic clove, grated
• 1 can cream corn
• 1 cup frozen corn
• Kosher salt
• Freshly ground black pepper

Directions:
1. Pour the cream cheese, 4 ounces of cotija cheese, tomatoes with chiles, mayonnaise, lime zest and juice, one 8-ounce package Mexican cheese blend, garlic, cream corn, and frozen corn in the pot. Season with salt and pepper and stir. Close crisping lid.

2. Select BAKE/ROAST, set temperature to 375°F, and set time to 20 minutes. Select START/STOP to begin.

3. After 10 minutes, open lid and sprinkle the dip with the remaining 2 ounces of cotija cheese and remaining 8-ounce package of Mexican blend cheese. Close crisping lid and continue cooking.

4. When cooking is complete, the cheese will be melted and the dip hot and bubbling at the edges. Open lid

and let the dip cool for 5 to 10 minutes before serving. Serve topped with chopped cilantro, hot sauce, and chili powder, if desired.

Nutrition Info:
• Calories: 538,Total Fat: 45g,Sodium: 807mg,Carbohydrates: 18g,Protein: 20g.

Crispy Chicken Skin

Servings: 7
Cooking Time: 10 Minutes

Ingredients:
• 1 teaspoon red chili flakes
• 1 teaspoon black pepper
• 1 teaspoon salt
• 9 ounces of chicken skin
• 2 tablespoons butter
• 1 teaspoon olive oil
• 1 teaspoon paprika

Directions:
1. Combine the black pepper, chilli flakes, and paprika together.
2. Stir the mixture and combine it with the chicken skin.
3. Let the mixture rest for 5 minutes. Set the Ninja Foodi's insert to" Sauté" mode.
4. Add the butter to the Ninja Foodi's insert and melt it.
5. Add the chicken skin and sauté it for 10 minutes, stirring frequently.
6. Once the chicken skin gets crunchy, remove it from the Ninja Foodi's insert.
7. Place the chicken skin on the paper towel and drain.
8. Serve warm.

Nutrition Info:
• Calories: 134; Fat: 11.5g; Carbohydrates: 0.98g; Protein: 7g

Strawberry Snack Bars

Servings: 16
Cooking Time: 30 Minutes

Ingredients:
• Butter flavored cooking spray
• 1 cup butter, soft
• 2 oz. stevia
• 1 tbsp. sour cream, reduced fat
• 1 egg
• 1 cup flour
• 1 cup whole wheat flour
• 1 cup strawberry jam, sugar free
• 1 tbsp. brown sugar
• 2 tbsp. walnuts, chopped

Directions:
1. Spray an 8-inch square pan with cooking spray.
2. In a medium bowl, beat butter and Stevia until creamy.
3. Beat in sour cream and egg until combined.
4. Stir in both flours, ½ cup at a time, until mixture forms a soft dough.
5. Press half the dough in the bottom of the prepared pan. Spread the jam over the top. Then spread the other half of the dough gently over the top. Sprinkle the brown sugar and nuts over the top.
6. Place the rack in the cooking pot and place the pan on it. Add the tender-crisp lid and set to bake on 375°F. Bake 25-30 minutes until bubbly and golden brown.
7. Transfer to wire rack to cool before cutting.

Nutrition Info:
• Calories 195,Total Fat 13g,Total Carbs 22g,Protein 3g,Sodium 97mg.

Steak And Minty Cheese

Servings: 4
Cooking Time: 15 Min

Ingredients:
• 2 New York strip steaks
• 8 oz. halloumi cheese /240g
• 12 kalamata olives
• Juice and zest of 1 lemon
• Olive oil
• 2 tbsp chopped parsley /30g
• 2 tbsp chopped mint /30g
• Salt and pepper, to taste

Directions:
1. Season the steaks with salt and pepper, and gently brush with olive oil. Place into the Ninja Foodi, close the crisping lid and cook for 6 minutes (for medium rare) on Air Crisp mode at 350 °F or 177°C. When ready, remove to a plate and set aside.
2. Drizzle the cheese with olive oil and place it in the Ninja Foodi; cook for 4 minutes.
3. Remove to a serving platter and serve with sliced steaks and olives, sprinkled with herbs, and lemon zest and juice.

Pistachio Stuffed Mushrooms

Servings: 8
Cooking Time: 20 Minutes

Ingredients:
- 16 large mushrooms
- 1 tbsp. olive oil
- ½ onion, diced fine
- ¼ cup unsalted pistachios, chopped
- 1/3 cup pretzels, crushed
- 2 tbsp. sour cream, fat free
- 2 tbsp. fresh parsley, chopped
- ¼ tsp pepper
- 1/8 tsp hot pepper sauce

Directions:
1. Remove stems from mushrooms and dice them.
2. Set cooker to sauté on medium heat. Add oil and let it get hot.
3. Add the chopped mushrooms, onions, and pistachios and cook, until vegetables are tender, about 2-4 minutes. Transfer to a large bowl.
4. Add the remaining ingredients to the mushroom mixture and mix well.
5. Wipe out the cooking pot and add the rack to it. Select the air fryer function on 350°F.
6. Stuff the mushroom caps with the filling. Lay a sheet of parchment paper over the top of the rack and place mushrooms on it.
7. Add the tender-crisp lid and bake 20-25 minutes or until mushrooms are tender. Serve.
8. Preheat oven to 350 °F. Remove mushroom stems from caps; finely chop stems.

Nutrition Info:
- Calories 84,Total Fat 4g,Total Carbs 11g,Protein 3g,Sodium 26mg.

Crispy Delicata Squash

Servings:4
Cooking Time: 15 Minutes

Ingredients:
- 1 large delicata squash, seeds removed and sliced
- 1 tablespoon extra-virgin olive oil
- ¼ teaspoon sea salt

Directions:
1. Place Cook & Crisp Basket in pot. Close crisping lid. Select AIR CRISP, set temperature to 390°F, and set time to 5 minutes. Select START/STOP to begin preheating.
2. In a large bowl, toss the squash with the olive oil and season with salt.
3. Once unit has preheated, place the squash in the basket. Close crisping lid.
4. Select AIR CRISP, set temperature to 390°F, and set time to 15 minutes. Select START/STOP to begin.
5. After 7 minutes, open the lid, then lift the basket and shake the squash. Lower the basket back into pot. Close lid and continue cooking until the squash achieves your desired crispiness.

Nutrition Info:
- Calories: 75,Total Fat: 4g,Sodium: 117mg,Carbohydrates: 10g,Protein: 2g.

Mini Crab Cakes

Servings: 9
Cooking Time: 10 Minutes

Ingredients:
- Nonstick cooking spray
- 2/3 cup Italian seasoned bread crumbs
- ½ cup egg substitute
- ½ red bell pepper, chopped fine
- ½ red onion, chopped fine
- 1 stalk celery, chopped fine
- 3 tbsp. lite mayonnaise
- 2 tsp fresh lemon juice
- ½ tsp salt
- ¾ tsp pepper
- 1 tsp dried tarragon
- 2 cans lump crabmeat, drained

Directions:
1. Lightly spray fryer basket with cooking spray.
2. In a large bowl, combine all ingredients, except crab, until combined. Gently fold in crab. Form into 36 patties. Place them in a single layer in the fryer basket without overcrowding them.
3. Add the tender-crisp lid and set to air fry on 350°F. Cook patties 3-5 minutes per side until golden brown. Repeat with remaining patties. Serve warm.

Nutrition Info:
- Calories 96,Total Fat 2g,Total Carbs 8g,Protein 10g,Sodium 543mg.

Potato Samosas

Servings:4
Cooking Time: 31 Minutes

Ingredients:

• 2 tablespoons canola oil
• 4 cups Russet potatoes, peeled and cut into ½-inch cubes
• 1 small yellow onion, diced
• 1 cup frozen peas
• 1½ teaspoons kosher salt
• 2½ teaspoons curry powder
• 1 cup vegetable stock
• 1 (½ package) frozen puff pastry sheet, thawed
• 1 egg beaten with 1 teaspoon water

Directions:

1. Select SEAR/SAUTÉ and set temperature to HI. Select START/STOP to begin. Let preheat for 5 minutes.
2. Add the oil and let heat for 1 minute. Add the potatoes, onions, and peas and cook, stirring frequently, about 10 minutes. Add the salt and curry powder and stir to coat the vegetables with it. Add the vegetable stock. Assemble pressure lid, making sure the pressure release valve is in the SEAL position.
3. Select PRESSURE and set to LO. Set time to 1 minute. Select START/STOP to begin.
4. When pressure cooking is complete, quick release the pressure by turning the pressure release valve to the VENT position. Carefully remove the lid when the unit has finished releasing pressure.
5. Transfer the potato mixture to a medium bowl. Let fully cool, about 15 minutes.
6. Lay out the puff pastry sheet on a cutting board. Using a rolling pin, roll out the sheet into a 12-by-10-inch rectangle. Cut it in 4 strips lengthwise, then cut the strips into thirds for a total of 12 squares.
7. Place 2 tablespoons of potato mixture in center of a pastry square. Brush the egg wash onto edges, and then fold one corner to another to create a triangle. Use a fork to seal edges together. Repeat with the remaining potato mixture and pastry squares.
8. Insert Cook & Crisp Basket into unit. Close crisping lid. Select AIR CRISP, set temperature to 390°F, and set time to 20 minutes. Select START/STOP to begin. Let preheat for 5 minutes.
9. Once unit has preheated, working in batches, place 3 samosas in the basket. Close lid to begin cooking.
10. After 5 minutes, open lid and use silicone-tipped tongs to remove the samosas. Repeat with the remaining batches of samosas.
11. Once all samosas are cooked, serve immediately.

Nutrition Info:

• Calories: 449,Total Fat: 24g,Sodium: 639mg,Carbohydrates: 53g,Protein: 10g.

Glazed Walnuts

Servings: 4
Cooking Time: 4 Minutes

Ingredients:

• ⅓ cup of water
• 6 ounces walnuts
• 5 tablespoon Erythritol
• ½ teaspoon ground ginger
• 3tablespoons psyllium husk powder

Directions:

1. Combine Erythritol and water together in a mixing bowl.
2. Add ground ginger and stir the mixture until the erythritol is dissolved.
3. Transfer the walnuts to the Ninja Foodi's insert and add sweet liquid.
4. Close the Ninja Foodi's lid and cook the dish in the "Pressure" mode for 4 minutes.
5. Remove the walnuts from the Ninja Foodi's insert.
6. Dip the walnuts in the Psyllium husk powder and serve.

Nutrition Info:

• Calories: 286; Fat: 25.1g; Carbohydrates: 10.4g; Protein: 10.3g

Scalloped Potatoes

Servings: 6
Cooking Time: 5 Minutes

Ingredients:

• 5 potatoes, sliced thin
• 5 tbsp. butter
• 2 cloves garlic, diced fine
• 1 cup vegetable broth
• ¾ tsp salt
• ½ tsp pepper
• 1 ½ tsp fresh parsley, diced fine
• ¼ cup cheddar cheese, grated

Directions:

1. Place potatoes in the cooking pot. Sprinkle with

salt, pepper, and parsley, toss to coat.

2. Add butter, garlic, and broth to the potatoes.

3. Add the lid and select pressure cooking on high. Set timer to 5 minutes. When timer goes off use natural release to remove the lid.

4. Transfer potatoes to serving dish and top with grated cheese to garnish. Serve.

Nutrition Info:

• Calories 415,Total Fat 17g,Total Carbs 55g,Protein 12g,Sodium 587mg.

Crispy Onion Rings

Servings: 7
Cooking Time: 8 Minutes

Ingredients:

• 1 cup coconut flour
• 1 teaspoon salt
• ½ teaspoon basil
• 1 teaspoon oregano
• ½ teaspoon cayenne pepper
• 3 eggs
• 5 medium white onions
• 3 tablespoons sesame oil

Directions:

1. Combine the coconut flour, salt, basil, oregano, and cayenne pepper together in a mixing bowl.

2. Stir the coconut flour mixture gently. Add the eggs to another bowl and whisk them.

3. Peel the onions and cut them into thick rings.

4. Separate the onion rings and dip them into the egg mixture.

5. Pour the sesame oil in the Ninja Foodi's insert. Preheat it on the "Pressure" mode.

6. Dip the onion rings in the flour mixture. Transfer the onion rings to the Ninja Foodi's insert.

7. Sauté the onions for 2 minutes on each side.

8. Transfer the cooked rings to the paper towel and rest briefly.

9. Season with salt while hot and serve.

Nutrition Info:

• Calories: 180; Fat: 10.1g; Fiber 7.5g; Carbohydrates: 6.8g; Protein: 5.6g

Tangy Jicama Chips

Servings: 8
Cooking Time: 10 Minutes

Ingredients:

• Nonstick cooking spray
• 1 jicama, peeled & sliced very thin
• 2 tbsp. extra virgin olive oil
• 1 ½ tsp lemon pepper seasoning

Directions:

1. Lightly spray the fryer basket with cooking spray.

2. Place the sliced jicama in a large bowl. Drizzle oil over the top and sprinkle with lemon pepper. Toss well to coat.

3. Place chips, in batches, in the basket. Place in cooker and add the tender-crisp lid. Set to air fry on 350°F. Cook 10 minutes until golden brown and crips, turning over halfway through cooking time. Repeat with remaining jicama. Serve.

Nutrition Info:

• Calories 61,Total Fat 3g,Total Carbs 7g,Protein 1g,Sodium 3mg.

Spicy Black Bean Dip

Servings: 12
Cooking Time: 20 Minutes

Ingredients:

• 2 16 oz. cans black beans, rinsed & drained, divided
• 1 cup salsa, divided
• 1 tsp olive oil
• ¾ onion, diced fine
• 1 red bell pepper, diced fine
• 3 cloves garlic, diced fine
• 1 tbsp. cilantro
• 2 tsp cumin
• ¼ tsp salt
• ¼ cup cheddar cheese, reduced fat, grated
• 1 tomato, chopped

Directions:

1. Add 1 can beans and ¼ cup salsa to a food processor or blender. Pulse until smooth.

2. Set cooker to sauté on medium heat. Add oil and let it get hot.

3. Add the onion, pepper, and garlic and cook, stirring occasionally, 5-7 minutes, or until vegetables are tender.

4. Add the pureed bean mixture along with remaining ingredients except cheese and tomatoes, mix well.

Reduce heat to low and bring to a simmer. Let cook 5 minutes, stirring frequently.

5. Transfer dip to serving bowl and top with cheese and tomato. Serve immediately.

Nutrition Info:
• Calories 100,Total Fat 2g,Total Carbs 16g,Protein 6g,Sodium 511mg.

Green Bean Casserole

Servings:6
Cooking Time: 46 Minutes

Ingredients:
• 1 cup water
• 2 pounds fresh green beans, cleaned and trimmed
• 1 cup vegetable or chicken stock
• ½ cup milk
• 1 can condensed cream of mushroom soup
• 2 teaspoons soy sauce
• 2 cups fried onion strings, divided
• Kosher salt
• Freshly ground black pepper

Directions:
1. Pour the water into the pot. Place the Reversible Rack in the lower position in the pot and add the green beans. Assemble pressure lid, making sure the pressure release valve is in the SEAL position.
2. Select PRESSURE and set to HI. Set time to 5 minutes. Select START/STOP to begin.
3. When pressure cooking is complete, quick release the pressure by turning the pressure release valve to the VENT position. Carefully remove lid when the unit has finished releasing pressure.
4. Remove rack and green beans. Drain the water from the pot and return to base.
5. Add the stock, milk, condensed soup, and soy sauce and stir. Add the green beans and 1 cup of fried onions. Season with salt and pepper. Stir well. Top with the remaining 1 cup of onion strings. Close crisping lid.
6. Select BAKE/ROAST, set temperature to 375°F, and set time to 30 minutes. Select START/STOP to begin.
7. When cooking is complete, open lid. Let cool for 5 minutes before serving.

Nutrition Info:
• Calories: 342,Total Fat: 20g,Sodium: 679mg,Carbohydrates: 31g,Protein: 4g.

Herby Fish Skewers

Servings: 4
Cooking Time: 75 Min

Ingredients:
• 1 pound cod loin, boneless, skinless; cubed /450g
• 2 garlic cloves, grated
• 1 lemon, juiced and zested
• 1 lemon, cut in wedges to serve
• 3 tbsp olive oil /45ml
• 1 tsp dill; chopped /5g
• 1 tsp parsley; chopped /5g
• Salt to taste

Directions:
1. In a bowl, combine the olive oil, garlic, dill, parsley, salt, and lemon juice. Stir in the cod and place in the fridge to marinate for 1 hour. Thread the cod pieces onto halved skewers.
2. Arrange into the oiled Ninja Foodi basket; close the crisping lid and cook for 10 minutes at 390 °F or 199°C. Flip them over halfway through cooking. When ready, remove to a serving platter, scatter lemon zest and serve with wedges.

Cumin Baby Carrots

Servings: 4
Cooking Time: 25 Min

Ingredients:
• 1 ¼ lb. baby carrots /562.5g
• 1 handful cilantro; chopped
• 2 tbsp olive oil /30ml
• ½ tsp cumin powder /2.5g
• ½ tsp garlic powder /2.5g
• 1 tsp cumin seeds /5g
• 1 tsp salt /5g
• ½ tsp black pepper /2.5g

Directions:
1. Place the baby carrots in a large bowl. Add cumin seeds, cumin, olive oil, salt, garlic powder, and pepper, and stir to coat them well.
2. Put the carrots in the Ninja Foodi's basket, close the crisping lid and cook for 20 minutes on Roast mode at 370 °F or 188°C. Remove to a platter and sprinkle with chopped cilantro, to serve.

Cheesy Onion Dip

Servings: 8
Cooking Time: 15 Minutes

Ingredients:
- 8 oz. cream cheese, soft
- 1 cup Swiss cheese, grated
- 1 cup mayonnaise
- 1 cup onion, grated

Directions:
1. In a medium bowl, combine all ingredients and mix thoroughly. Transfer to a small baking dish and cover tightly with foil.
2. Place the trivet in the cooking pot along with 1 cup of water. Place the dish on trivet.
3. Secure the lid and select pressure cooking on high. Set timer for 15 minutes.
4. When timer goes off, use quick release to remove the lid.
5. Remove the foil and add the tender-crisp lid. Set to air fryer on 400°F cook 1-2 minutes until the top is golden brown. Serve warm.

Nutrition Info:
- Calories 352, Total Fat 35g, Total Carbs 3g, Protein 6g, Sodium 290mg.

Zesty Brussels Sprouts With Raisins

Servings: 4
Cooking Time: 45 Min

Ingredients:
- 14 oz. Brussels sprouts, steamed /420g
- 2 oz. toasted pine nuts /60g
- 2 oz. raisins /60g
- 1 tbsp olive oil/15ml
- Juice and zest of 1 orange

Directions:
1. Soak the raisins in the orange juice and let sit for about 20 minutes. Drizzle the Brussels sprouts with the olive oil, and place them in the basket of the Ninja Foodi.
2. Close the crisping lid and cook for 15 minutes on Air Crisp mode at 370 °F or 188°C. Remove to a bowl and top with pine nuts, raisins, and orange zest.

Sweet Potato Fries

Servings: 4
Cooking Time: 20 Minutes

Ingredients:
- Nonstick cooking spray
- ½ tsp cumin
- ½ tsp chili powder
- ½ tsp pepper
- ½ tsp salt
- ¼ tsp cayenne pepper
- 2 sweet potatoes, peeled & julienned
- 1 tbsp. extra-virgin olive oil

Directions:
1. Lightly spray fryer basket with cooking spray.
2. In a small bowl, combine cumin, chili powder, pepper, salt, and cayenne pepper.
3. Place potatoes in a large bowl and sprinkle spice mix and oil over them. Toss well to coat.
4. Place the fries, in small batches, in the basket and place in the cooking pot.
5. Add the tender-crisp lid and select air fryer on 425°F. Cook fries 15-20 minutes, until crispy on the outside and tender inside, turning halfway through cooking time. Serve immediately.

Nutrition Info:
- Calories 86, Total Fat 3g, Total Carbs 13g, Protein 1g, Sodium 327mg.

Soups & Stews

Chicken Enchilada Soup ..33

Goulash (hungarian Beef Soup) 33

Lasagna Soup 34

Roasted Tomato And Seafood Stew 34

Braised Pork And Black Bean Stew................................35

Chicken Noodle Soup.......35

Chicken Chili....................36

Chickpea, Spinach, And Sweet Potato Stew 36

Mushroom And Wild Rice Soup....................................37

Jamaican Jerk Chicken Stew 37

Chicken Potpie Soup 37

Chicken Tomatillo Stew ...38

Fish Chowder And Biscuits 39

Italian Sausage, Potato, And Kale Soup 39

Pho Tom...........................40

Loaded Potato Soup..........40

Creamy Pumpkin Soup.....41

Butternut Squash, Apple, Bacon And Orzo Soup 41

Tex-mex Chicken Tortilla Soup...................................42

Coconut And Shrimp Bisque 42

Chicken Enchilada Soup

Servings:8
Cooking Time: 30 Minutes

Ingredients:
- 1 tablespoon extra-virgin olive oil
- 1 small red onion, diced
- 2 cans fire-roasted tomatoes with chiles
- 1 can corn
- 1 can black beans, rinsed and drained
- 1 can red enchilada sauce
- 1 can tomato paste
- 3 tablespoons taco seasoning
- 2 tablespoons freshly squeezed lime juice
- 2 boneless, skinless chicken breasts
- Salt
- Freshly ground black pepper

Directions:
1. Select SEAR/SAUTÉ and set temperature to MD:HI. Select START/STOP to begin. Let preheat for 5 minutes.
2. Place the olive oil and onion in the pot. Cook until the onions are translucent, about 2 minutes.
3. Add the tomatoes, corn, beans, enchilada sauce, tomato paste, taco seasoning, lime juice, and chicken. Season with salt and pepper and stir. Assemble pressure lid, making sure the pressure release valve is in the SEAL position.
4. Select PRESSURE and set to HI. Set time to 9 minutes. Select START/STOP to begin.
5. When pressure cooking is complete, allow pressure to naturally release for 10 minutes. After 10 minutes, quick release remaining pressure by moving the pressure release valve to the VENT position. Carefully remove lid when unit has finished releasing pressure.
6. Transfer the chicken breasts to a cutting board. Using two forks, shred the chicken. Return the chicken back to the pot and stir. Serve in a bowl with toppings of choice, such as shredded cheese, crushed tortilla chips, sliced avocado, sour cream, cilantro, and lime wedges, if desired.

Nutrition Info:
- Calories: 257,Total Fat: 4g,Sodium: 819mg,Carbohydrates: 37g,Protein: 20g.

Goulash (hungarian Beef Soup)

Servings:6
Cooking Time: 55 Minutes

Ingredients:
- ½ cup all-purpose flour
- 1 tablespoon kosher salt
- ½ teaspoon freshly ground black pepper
- 2 pounds beef stew meat
- 2 tablespoons canola oil
- 1 medium red bell pepper, seeded and chopped
- 4 garlic cloves, minced
- 1 large yellow onion, diced
- 2 tablespoons smoked paprika
- 1½ pounds small Yukon Gold potatoes, halved
- 2 cups beef broth
- 2 tablespoons tomato paste
- ¼ cup sour cream
- Fresh parsley, for garnish

Directions:
1. Select SEAR/SAUTÉ and set to HI. Select START/STOP to begin. Let preheat for 5 minutes.
2. Mix together the flour, salt, and pepper in a small bowl. Dip the pieces of beef into the flour mixture, shaking off any extra flour.
3. Add the oil and let heat for 1 minute. Place the beef in the pot and brown it on all sides, about 10 minutes.
4. Add the bell pepper, garlic, onion, and smoked paprika. Sauté for about 8 minutes or until the onion is translucent.
5. Add the potatoes, beef broth, and tomato paste and stir. Assemble pressure lid, making sure the pressure release valve is in the SEAL position.
6. Select PRESSURE and set to LO. Set time to 30 minutes. Select START/STOP to begin.
7. When pressure cooking is complete, quick release the pressure by moving the pressure release valve to the VENT position. Carefully remove lid when unit has finished releasing pressure.
8. Add the sour cream and mix thoroughly. Garnish with parsley, if desired, and serve immediately.

Nutrition Info:
- Calories: 413,Total Fat: 13g,Sodium: 432mg,Carbohydrates: 64g,Protein: 37g.

Lasagna Soup

Servings:8
Cooking Time: 16 Minutes

Ingredients:
- 1 tablespoon extra-virgin olive oil
- 16 ounces Italian sausage
- 1 small onion, diced
- 4 garlic cloves, minced
- 1 jar marinara sauce
- 2 cups water
- 1 cup vegetable broth
- 1 teaspoon dried basil
- 1 teaspoon dried oregano
- ½ teaspoon dried thyme
- Freshly ground black pepper
- 8 ounces lasagna noodles, broken up
- 1 cup ricotta cheese
- ½ cup grated Parmesan cheese
- 1 teaspoon dried parsley
- ½ cup heavy (whipping) cream
- 1 cup shredded mozzarella cheese

Directions:
1. Select SEAR/SAUTÉ and set to HI. Select START/ STOP to begin. Let preheat for 5 minutes.
2. Add the oil and sausage and cook for about 5 minutes. Using a wooden spoon, break apart the sausage and stir.
3. Add the onions and cook, stirring occasionally, for 3 minutes. Add the garlic and cook for 2 minutes, or until the meat is no longer pink.
4. Add the marinara sauce, water, vegetable broth, basil, oregano, thyme, pepper, and lasagna noodles. Assemble pressure lid, making sure the pressure release valve is in the SEAL position.
5. Select PRESSURE and set to HI. Set time to 6 minutes. Select START/STOP to begin.
6. In a medium bowl, combine the ricotta cheese, Parmesan cheese, and parsley. Cover and refrigerate.
7. When pressure cooking is complete, quick release the pressure by turning the pressure release valve to the VENT position. Carefully remove lid when unit has finished releasing pressure.
8. Stir in the heavy cream. Add the cheese mixture and stir. Top the soup with the mozzarella. Close crisping lid.
9. Select BROIL and set time to 5 minutes. Select START/STOP to begin.
10. When cooking is complete, serve immediately.

Nutrition Info:
- Calories: 398,Total Fat: 22g,Sodium: 892mg,Carbohydrates: 29g,Protein: 23g.

Roasted Tomato And Seafood Stew

Servings:6
Cooking Time: 46 Minutes

Ingredients:
- 2 tablespoons extra-virgin olive oil
- 1 yellow onion, diced
- 1 fennel bulb, tops removed and bulb diced
- 3 garlic cloves, minced
- 1 cup dry white wine
- 2 cans fire-roasted tomatoes
- 2 cups chicken stock
- 1 pound medium shrimp, peeled and deveined
- 1 pound raw white fish (cod or haddock), cubed
- Salt
- Freshly ground black pepper
- Fresh basil, torn, for garnish

Directions:
1. Select SEAR/SAUTÉ and set to MED. Select START/STOP to begin. Let preheat for 3 minutes.
2. Add the olive oil, onions, fennel, and garlic. Cook for about 3 minutes, until translucent.
3. Add the white wine and deglaze, scraping any stuck bits from the bottom of the pot using a silicone spatula. Add the roasted tomatoes and chicken stock. Simmer for 25 to 30 minutes. Add the shrimp and white fish.
4. Select SEAR/SAUTÉ and set to MD:LO. Select START/STOP to begin.
5. Simmer for 10 minutes, stirring frequently, until the shrimp and fish are cooked through. Season with salt and pepper.
6. Ladle into bowl and serve topped with torn basil.

Nutrition Info:
- Calories: 301,Total Fat: 8g,Sodium: 808mg,Carbohydrates: 21g,Protein: 26g.

Braised Pork And Black Bean Stew

Servings:8
Cooking Time: 30 Minutes

Ingredients:
- 2 pounds boneless pork shoulder, cut into 1-inch pieces
- ¼ cup all-purpose flour
- ¼ cup unsalted butter
- ½ small onion, diced
- 1 carrot, diced
- 1 celery stalk, diced
- 2 garlic cloves, minced
- 1 tablespoon tomato paste
- 1 tablespoon cumin
- 1 tablespoon smoked paprika
- 4 cups chicken stock
- 1 can diced tomatoes with chiles
- 1 can black beans, rinsed and drained
- 1 can hominy, rinsed and drained
- Sea salt
- Freshly ground black pepper

Directions:
1. In a large bowl, coat the pork pieces with the flour.
2. Select SEAR/SAUTÉ and set to HI. Select START/STOP to begin. Let preheat for 5 minutes.
3. Add the butter. Once melted, add the pork and sear for 5 minutes, turning the pieces so they begin to brown on all sides.
4. Add the onion, carrot, celery, garlic, tomato paste, cumin, and paprika and cook, stirring occasionally, for 3 minutes.
5. Add the chicken stock and tomatoes. Assemble pressure lid, making sure the pressure release valve is in the SEAL position.
6. Select PRESSURE and set to HI. Set time to 15 minutes. Select START/STOP to begin.
7. When pressure cooking is complete, quick release the pressure by turning the pressure release valve to the VENT position. Carefully remove lid when the unit has finished releasing pressure.
8. Select SEAR/SAUTÉ and set to HI. Select START/STOP to begin.
9. Whisk in the beans and hominy. Season with salt and pepper and cook for 2 minutes. Serve.

Nutrition Info:
- Calories: 342,Total Fat: 12g,Sodium: 638mg,Carbohydrates: 27g,Protein: 29g.

Chicken Noodle Soup

Servings:8
Cooking Time: 19 Minutes

Ingredients:
- 2 tablespoons unsalted butter
- 1 large onion, chopped
- 2 carrots, chopped
- 2 celery stalks, chopped
- 2 pounds boneless chicken breast
- 4 cups chicken broth
- 4 cups water
- 1 tablespoon chopped fresh parsley
- 1 teaspoon dried thyme
- 1 teaspoon dried oregano
- ½ teaspoon sea salt
- ½ teaspoon freshly ground black pepper
- 5 ounces egg noodles

Directions:
1. Select SEAR/SAUTÉ and set to HI. Select START/STOP to begin. Let preheat for 5 minutes.
2. Add the butter. Once melted, add the onion, carrots, and celery. Cook, stirring occasionally, for 5 minutes.
3. Add the chicken, chicken broth, water, parsley, thyme, oregano, salt, and pepper. Assemble pressure lid, making sure the pressure release valve is in the SEAL position.
4. Select PRESSURE and set to HI. Set time to 8 minutes. Select START/STOP to begin.
5. When pressure cooking is complete, quick release the pressure by moving the pressure release valve to the VENT position. Carefully remove lid when unit has finished releasing pressure.
6. Remove the chicken from the soup and shred it with two forks. Set aside.
7. Add the egg noodles. Select SEAR/SAUTÉ and set to MED. Select START/STOP to begin.
8. Cook for 6 minutes, uncovered, or until the noodles are tender. Stir the shredded chicken back into the pot. Serve.

Nutrition Info:
- Calories: 237,Total Fat: 5g,Sodium: 413mg,Carbohydrates: 17g,Protein: 30g.

Chicken Chili

Servings:8
Cooking Time: 30 Minutes

Ingredients:
- 1 tablespoon extra-virgin olive oil
- 1 yellow onion, chopped
- 4 garlic cloves, minced
- 2 pounds boneless chicken breast, cut in half crosswise
- 4 cups chicken broth
- 1 green bell pepper, seeded and chopped
- 2 jalapeños, seeded and chopped
- 1½ tablespoons ground cumin
- 1 tablespoon coriander
- 1 teaspoon dried oregano
- 1 teaspoon sea salt
- 1 teaspoon freshly ground black pepper
- 2 cans cannellini beans, rinsed and drained
- Shredded Monterey Jack cheese, for garnish
- Chopped cilantro, for garnish
- Lime wedge, for garnish

Directions:
1. Select SEAR/SAUTÉ and set to HI. Select START/STOP to begin. Let preheat for 5 minutes.
2. Add the oil and onions and cook, stirring occasionally, for 3 minutes. Add the garlic and cook for 2 minutes.
3. Add the chicken breast, chicken broth, green bell pepper, jalapeño, cumin, coriander, oregano, salt, and black pepper. Assemble pressure lid, making sure the pressure release valve is in the SEAL position.
4. Select PRESSURE and set to HI. Set time to 15 minutes. Select START/STOP to begin.
5. When pressure cooking is complete, quick release the pressure by turning the pressure release valve to the VENT position. Carefully remove lid when unit has finished releasing pressure.
6. Remove the chicken from the soup and shred it using two forks. Set aside.
7. Add the cannellini beans. Select SEAR/SAUTÉ and set to MED. Select START/STOP to begin. Cook until heated through, about 5 minutes.
8. Add shredded chicken back to the pot. Serve, garnished with the cheese, cilantro, and lime wedge (if using).

Nutrition Info:
- Calories: 279,Total Fat: 9g,Sodium: 523mg,Carbohydrates: 18g,Protein: 32g.

Chickpea, Spinach, And Sweet Potato Stew

Servings:6
Cooking Time: 23 Minutes

Ingredients:
- 1 tablespoon extra-virgin olive oil
- 1 yellow onion, diced
- 4 garlic cloves, minced
- 4 sweet potatoes, peeled and diced
- 4 cups vegetable broth
- 1 can fire-roasted diced tomatoes, undrained
- 2 cans chickpeas, drained
- 1½ teaspoons ground cumin
- 1 teaspoon ground coriander
- ½ teaspoon paprika
- ½ teaspoon sea salt
- ½ teaspoon freshly ground black pepper
- 4 cups baby spinach

Directions:
1. Select SEAR/SAUTÉ and set to MD:HI. Select START/STOP to begin. Allow the pot to preheat for 5 minutes.
2. Combine the oil, onion, and garlic in the pot. Cook, stirring occasionally, for 5 minutes.
3. Add the sweet potatoes, vegetable broth, tomatoes, chickpeas, cumin, coriander, paprika, salt, and black pepper to the pot. Assemble the pressure lid, making sure the pressure release valve is in the SEAL position.
4. Select PRESSURE and set to HI. Set the time to 8 minutes, then select START/STOP to begin.
5. When pressure cooking is complete, quick release the pressure by moving the pressure release valve to the VENT position. Carefully remove the lid when the unit has finished releasing pressure.
6. Add the spinach to the pot and stir until wilted. Serve.

Nutrition Info:
- Calories: 220,Total Fat: 4g,Sodium: 593mg,Carbohydrates: 42g,Protein: 7g.

Mushroom And Wild Rice Soup

Servings:6
Cooking Time: 30 Minutes

Ingredients:
- 5 medium carrots, chopped
- 5 celery stalks, chopped
- 1 onion, chopped
- 3 garlic cloves, minced
- 1 cup wild rice
- 8 ounces fresh mushrooms, sliced
- 6 cups vegetable broth
- 1 teaspoon kosher salt
- 1 teaspoon poultry seasoning
- ½ teaspoon dried thyme

Directions:
1. Place all the ingredients in the pot. Assemble pressure lid, making sure the pressure release valve is in the SEAL position.
2. Select PRESSURE and set to HI. Set time to 30 minutes. Select START/STOP to begin.
3. When pressure cooking is complete, quick release the pressure by turning the pressure release valve to the VENT position. Carefully remove lid when unit has finished releasing pressure.
4. Serve.

Nutrition Info:
- Calories: 175,Total Fat: 2g,Sodium: 723mg,Carbohydrates: 30g,Protein: 11g.

Jamaican Jerk Chicken Stew

Servings:6
Cooking Time: 28 Minutes

Ingredients:
- 2 tablespoons canola oil
- 6 boneless, skinless chicken thighs, cut in 2-inch
- pieces
- 2 tablespoons Jamaican jerk spice
- 1 white onion, peeled and chopped
- 2 red bell peppers, chopped
- ½ head green cabbage, core removed and cut into 2-inch pieces
- 1½ cups wild rice blend, rinsed
- 4 cups chicken stock
- ½ cup prepared Jamaican jerk sauce
- Kosher salt

Directions:
1. Select SEAR/SAUTÉ and set to HI. Select START/STOP to begin. Let preheat for 5 minutes.
2. Add the oil, chicken, and jerk spice and stir. Cook for 5 minutes, stirring occasionally.
3. Add the onions, bell pepper, and cabbage and stir. Cook for 5 minutes, stirring occasionally.
4. Add the wild rice and stock, stirring well to combine. Assemble pressure lid, making sure the pressure release valve is in the SEAL position.
5. Select PRESSURE and set to HI. Set time to 18 minutes. Select START/STOP to begin.
6. When pressure cooking is complete, allow pressure to naturally release for 10 minutes. After 10 minutes, quick release any remaining pressure by moving the pressure release valve to the VENT position. Carefully remove lid when unit has finished releasing pressure.
7. Add the jerk sauce to pot, stirring well to combine. Let the stew sit for 5 minutes, allowing it to thicken. Season with salt and serve.

Nutrition Info:
- Calories: 404,Total Fat: 10g,Sodium: 373mg,Carbohydrates: 53g,Protein: 29g.

Chicken Potpie Soup

Servings:6
Cooking Time: 1 Hour

Ingredients:
- 4 chicken breasts
- 2 cups chicken stock
- 2 tablespoons unsalted butter
- 1 yellow onion, diced
- 16 ounces frozen mixed vegetables
- 1 cup heavy (whipping) cream
- 1 can condensed cream of chicken soup
- 2 tablespoons cornstarch
- 2 tablespoons water
- Salt
- Freshly ground black pepper
- 1 tube refrigerated biscuit dough

Directions:
1. Place the chicken and stock in the pot. Assemble pressure lid, making sure the pressure release valve is in the SEAL position.
2. Select PRESSURE and set to HI. Set time to 15 minutes. Select START/STOP to begin.
3. Once pressure cooking is complete, quick release the pressure by turning the pressure release valve to the VENT position. Carefully remove lid when the unit has finished releasing pressure.

4. Using a silicone-tipped utensil, shred the chicken.

5. Select SEAR/SAUTÉ and set to MED. Add the butter, onion, mixed vegetables, cream, and condensed soup and stir. Select START/STOP to begin. Simmer for 10 minutes.

6. In a small bowl, whisk together the cornstarch and water. Slowly whisk the cornstarch mixture into the soup. Set temperature to LO and simmer for 10 minutes more. Season with salt and pepper.

7. Carefully arrange the biscuits on top of the simmering soup. Close crisping lid.

8. Select BAKE/ROAST, set temperature to 325°F, and set time to 15 minutes. Select START/STOP to begin.

9. When cooking is complete, remove the biscuits. To serve, place a biscuit in a bowl and ladle soup over it.

Nutrition Info:

• Calories: 731, Total Fat: 26g, Sodium: 1167mg, Carbohydrates: 56g, Protein: 45g.

Chicken Tomatillo Stew

Servings: 4

Cooking Time: 46 Minutes

Ingredients:

• 3 medium onions, quartered
• 3 garlic cloves, whole
• 2 poblano peppers, seeded and quartered
• ½ pound tomatillos
• 2 small jalapeño peppers, seeded and quartered (optional)
• 2 tablespoons canola oil, divided
• Kosher salt
• Freshly ground black pepper
• 2½ pounds boneless, skinless chicken thighs
• 1 cup chicken stock
• 1 teaspoon cumin
• 1 tablespoon oregano
• 1 tablespoon all-purpose flour
• 1 cup water

Directions:

1. Place Cook & Crisp Basket in pot and close crisping lid. Select AIR CRISP and set to HIGH. Set time to 25 minutes. Select START/STOP to begin. Let preheat for 5 minutes.

2. Place the onions, garlic, poblano peppers, tomatillos, jalapeños, 1 tablespoon of canola oil, salt, and pepper in a medium-sized bowl and mix until vegetables are evenly coated.

3. Once unit has preheated, open lid and place the vegetables in the basket. Close lid and cook for 20 minutes.

4. After 10 minutes, open lid, then lift basket and shake the vegetables or toss them with silicone-tipped tongs. Lower basket back into pot and close lid to continue cooking.

5. When cooking is complete, remove basket and vegetables and set aside.

6. Select SEAR/SAUTÉ and set to HI. Select START/STOP to begin. Let preheat for 5 minutes.

7. Season the chicken thighs with salt and pepper.

8. After 5 minutes, add the remaining 1 tablespoon of oil and chicken. Sear the chicken, about 3 minutes on each side.

9. Add the chicken stock, cumin, and oregano. Scrape the pot with a rubber or wooden spoon to release any pieces that are sticking to the bottom. Assemble pressure lid, making sure the pressure release valve is in the SEAL position.

10. Select PRESSURE and set to HI. Set time to 10 minutes. Select START/STOP to begin.

11. Remove the vegetables from the basket and roughly chop.

12. In a small bowl, add the flour and water and stir.

13. When pressure cooking is complete, quick release the pressure by turning the pressure release valve to the VENT position. Carefully remove lid when unit has finished releasing pressure.

14. Remove the chicken and shred it using two forks.

15. Select SEAR/SAUTÉ and set to MED. Select START/STOP to begin. Return the chicken and vegetables and stir with a rubber or wooden spoon, being sure to scrape the bottom of the pot. Slowly stir in the flour mixture. Bring to a simmer and cook for 10 minutes, or until the broth becomes clear and has thickened.

16. When cooking is complete, serve as is or garnish with sour cream, lime, cilantro, and a flour tortilla for dipping.

Nutrition Info:

• Calories: 487, Total Fat: 20g, Sodium: 382mg, Carbohydrates: 19g, Protein: 59g.

Fish Chowder And Biscuits

Servings: 8
Cooking Time: 30 Minutes

Ingredients:
- 5 strips bacon, sliced
- 1 white onion, chopped
- 3 celery stalks, chopped
- 4 cups chicken stock
- 2 Russet potatoes, rinsed and cut in 1-inch pieces
- 4 frozen haddock fillets
- Kosher salt
- ½ cup clam juice
- ⅓ cup all-purpose flour
- 2 cans evaporated milk
- 1 tube refrigerated biscuit dough

Directions:
1. Select SEAR/SAUTÉ and set to HI. Select START/STOP to begin. Let preheat for 5 minutes.
2. Add the bacon and cook, stirring frequently, for 5 minutes. Add the onion and celery and cook for an additional 5 minutes, stirring occasionally.
3. Add the chicken stock, potatoes, and haddock filets. Season with salt. Assemble pressure lid, making sure the pressure release valve is in the SEAL position.
4. Select PRESSURE and set to HI. Set time to 5 minutes. Select START/STOP to begin.
5. Whisk together the clam juice and flour in a small bowl, ensuring there are no flour clumps in the mixture.
6. When pressure cooking is complete, quick release the pressure by moving the pressure release valve to the VENT position. Carefully remove lid when unit has finished releasing pressure.
7. Select SEAR/SAUTÉ and set to MED. Select START/STOP to begin. Add the clam juice mixture, stirring well to combine. Add the evaporated milk and continue to stir frequently for 3 to 5 minutes, until chowder has thickened to your desired texture.
8. Place the Reversible Rack in the pot in the higher position. Place the biscuits on the rack; it may be necessary to tear the last biscuit or two into smaller pieces in order to fit them all on the rack. Close crisping lid.
9. Select BAKE/ROAST, set temperature to 350°F, and set time to 12 minutes. Select START/STOP to begin.
10. After 10 minutes, check the biscuits for doneness. If desired, cook for up to an additional 2 minutes.
11. When cooking is complete, open lid and remove rack from pot. Serve the chowder and top each portion with biscuits.

Nutrition Info:
- Calories: 518, Total Fat: 22g, Sodium: 1189mg, Carbohydrates: 49g, Protein: 33g.

Italian Sausage, Potato, And Kale Soup

Servings: 8
Cooking Time: 18 Minutes

Ingredients:
- 1 tablespoon extra-virgin olive oil
- 1½ pounds hot Italian sausage, ground
- 1 pound sweet Italian sausage, ground
- 1 large yellow onion, diced
- 2 tablespoons minced garlic
- 4 large Russet potatoes, cut in ½-inch thick quarters
- 5 cups chicken stock
- 2 tablespoons Italian seasoning
- 2 teaspoons crushed red pepper flakes
- Salt
- Freshly ground black pepper
- 6 cups kale, chopped
- ½ cup heavy (whipping) cream

Directions:
1. Select SEAR/SAUTÉ. Set temperature to MD:HI. Select START/STOP to begin. Let preheat for 5 minutes.
2. Add the olive oil and hot and sweet Italian sausage. Cook, breaking up the sausage with a spatula, until the meat is cooked all the way through, about 5 minutes.
3. Add the onion, garlic, potatoes, chicken stock, Italian seasoning, and crushed red pepper flakes. Season with salt and pepper. Stir to combine. Assemble pressure lid, making sure the pressure release valve is in the SEAL position.
4. Select PRESSURE and set to HI. Set time to 10 minutes. Select START/STOP to begin.
5. When pressure cooking is complete, quick release the pressure by turning the pressure release valve to the VENT position. Carefully remove lid when the unit has finished releasing pressure.
6. Stir in the kale and heavy cream. Serve.

Nutrition Info:
- Calories: 689, Total Fat: 45g, Sodium: 1185mg, Carbohydrates: 38g, Protein: 33g.

Pho Tom

Servings:6
Cooking Time: 36 Minutes

Ingredients:
- 2 tablespoons canola oil
- 1 onion, peeled and halved
- 1 piece fresh ginger, peeled
- 2 tablespoons brown sugar
- 2 tablespoons kosher salt
- 1½ tablespoons Chinese five-spice powder
- ¼ cup fish sauce
- 4 cups beef bone broth
- 8 cups water
- 1 package rice noodles, cooked according to the package directions
- 1 pound peeled cooked shrimp
- Bean sprouts, for topping (optional)
- Lime wedges, for serving (optional)
- Fresh basil, for topping (optional)
- Sriracha, for topping (optional)

Directions:
1. Select SEAR/SAUTÉ and set temperature to HI. Select START/STOP to begin. Allow to preheat for 5 minutes.
2. Add oil to the pot and allow to heat for 1 minute. Add the onion and ginger and sear on all sides, about 6 minutes. Select START/STOP to end the function.
3. Add the sugar, salt, five-spice powder, fish sauce, bone broth, and water. Stir for 1 minute to combine.
4. Assemble the pressure lid, making sure the pressure release valve is in the SEAL position.
5. Select PRESSURE and set to HI. Set the time to 30 minutes. Select START/STOP to begin.
6. When pressure cooking is complete, quick release the pressure by turning the pressure release valve to the VENT position. Carefully remove the lid when the unit has finished releasing pressure.
7. Add the desired amount of noodles to a bowl and top with 5 or 6 shrimp and some sliced onion. Ladle the pho broth to cover the noodles, shrimp, and onion. Top as desired.

Nutrition Info:
- Calories: 242,Total Fat: 7g,Sodium: 2419mg,Carbohydrates: 25g,Protein: 22g.

Loaded Potato Soup

Servings:6
Cooking Time: 30 Minutes

Ingredients:
- 5 slices bacon, chopped
- 1 onion, chopped
- 3 garlic cloves, minced
- 4 pounds Russet potatoes, peeled and chopped
- 4 cups chicken broth
- 1 cup whole milk
- ½ teaspoon sea salt
- ½ teaspoon freshly ground black pepper
- 1½ cups shredded Cheddar cheese
- Sour cream, for serving (optional)
- Chopped fresh chives, for serving (optional)

Directions:
1. Select SEAR/SAUTÉ and set to HI. Select START/STOP to begin. Let preheat for 5 minutes.
2. Add the bacon, onion, and garlic. Cook, stirring occasionally, for 5 minutes. Set aside some of the bacon for garnish.
3. Add the potatoes and chicken broth. Assemble pressure lid, making sure the pressure release valve is in the SEAL position.
4. Select PRESSURE and set to HI. Set time to 10 minutes, then select START/STOP to begin.
5. When pressure cooking is complete, quick release the pressure by moving the pressure release valve to the VENT position. Carefully remove lid when unit has finished releasing pressure.
6. Add the milk and mash the ingredients until the soup reaches your desired consistency. Season with the salt and black pepper. Sprinkle the cheese evenly over the top of the soup. Close crisping lid.
7. Select BROIL and set time to 5 minutes. Select START/STOP to begin.
8. When cooking is complete, top with the reserved crispy bacon and serve with sour cream and chives (if using).

Nutrition Info:
- Calories: 468,Total Fat: 19g,Sodium: 1041mg,Carbohydrates: 53g,Protein: 23g.

Creamy Pumpkin Soup

Servings:8
Cooking Time: 23 Minutes

Ingredients:
- ¼ cup unsalted butter
- ½ small onion, diced
- 1 celery stalk, diced
- 1 carrot, diced
- 2 garlic cloves, minced
- 1 can pumpkin purée
- 1½ teaspoons poultry spice blend
- 3 cups chicken stock
- 1 package cream cheese
- 1 cup heavy (whipping) cream
- ¼ cup maple syrup
- Sea salt
- Freshly ground black pepper

Directions:
1. Select SEAR/SAUTÉ and set to HI. Select START/ STOP to begin. Let preheat for 5 minutes.
2. Add the butter. Once melted, add the onions, celery, carrot, and garlic. Cook, stirring occasionally, for 3 minutes
3. Add the pumpkin, poultry spice, and chicken stock. Assemble pressure lid, making sure the pressure release valve is in the SEAL position.
4. Select PRESSURE and set to HI. Set time to 15 minutes. Select START/STOP to begin.
5. When pressure cooking is complete, quick release the pressure by turning the pressure release valve to the VENT position. Carefully remove lid when the unit has finished releasing pressure.
6. Whisk in the cream cheese, heavy cream, and maple syrup. Season with salt and pepper. Using an immersion blender, purée the soup until smooth.

Nutrition Info:
- Calories: 334,Total Fat: 28g,Sodium: 266mg,Carbohydrates: 17g,Protein: 6g.

Butternut Squash, Apple, Bacon And Orzo Soup

Servings:8
Cooking Time: 28 Minutes

Ingredients:
- 4 slices uncooked bacon, cut into ½-inch pieces
- 12 ounces butternut squash, peeled and cubed
- 1 green apple, cut into small cubes
- Kosher salt
- Freshly ground black pepper
- 1 tablespoon minced fresh oregano
- 2 quarts chicken stock
- 1 cup orzo

Directions:
1. Select SEAR/SAUTÉ and set temperature to HI. Select START/STOP to begin. Let preheat for 5 minutes.
2. Place the bacon in the pot and cook, stirring frequently, about 5 minutes, or until fat is rendered and the bacon starts to brown. Using a slotted spoon, transfer the bacon to a paper towel-lined plate to drain, leaving the rendered bacon fat in the pot.
3. Add the butternut squash, apple, salt, and pepper and sauté until partially soft, about 5 minutes. Stir in the oregano.
4. Add the bacon back into the pot along with the chicken stock. Bring to a boil for about 10 minutes, then add the orzo. Cook for about 8 minutes, until the orzo is tender. Serve.

Nutrition Info:
- Calories: 247,Total Fat: 7g,Sodium: 563mg,Carbohydrates: 33g,Protein: 12g.

Tex-mex Chicken Tortilla Soup

Servings:8
Cooking Time: 20 Minutes

Ingredients:

- 1 tablespoon extra-virgin olive oil
- 1 onion, chopped
- 1 pound boneless, skinless chicken breasts
- 6 cups chicken broth
- 1 jar salsa
- 4 ounces tomato paste
- 1 tablespoon chili powder
- 2 teaspoons cumin
- ½ teaspoon sea salt
- ½ teaspoon freshly ground black pepper
- 1 pinch of cayenne pepper
- 1 can black beans, rinsed and drained
- 2 cups frozen corn
- Tortilla strips, for garnish

Directions:

1. Select SEAR/SAUTÉ and set to temperature to HI. Select START/STOP to begin. Let preheat for 5 minutes.
2. Place the olive oil and onions into the pot and cook, stirring occasionally, for 5 minutes.
3. Add the chicken breast, chicken broth, salsa, tomato paste, chili powder, cumin, salt, pepper, and cayenne pepper. Assemble pressure lid, making sure the pressure release valve is in the SEAL position.
4. Select PRESSURE and set to HI. Set time to 10 minutes. Select START/STOP to begin.
5. When pressure cooking is complete, allow pressure to naturally release for 10 minutes. After 10 minutes, quick release remaining pressure by moving the pressure release valve to the VENT position. Carefully remove lid when unit has finished releasing pressure.
6. Transfer the chicken breasts to a cutting board and shred with two forks. Set aside.
7. Add the black beans and corn. Select SEAR/SAUTÉ and set to MD. Select START/STOP to begin. Cook until heated through, about 5 minutes.
8. Add shredded chicken back to the pot. Garnish with tortilla strips, serve, and enjoy!

Nutrition Info:

- Calories: 186,Total Fat: 4g,Sodium: 783mg,Carbohydrates: 23g,Protein: 19g.

Coconut And Shrimp Bisque

Servings:4
Cooking Time: 15 Minutes

Ingredients:

- ¼ cup red curry paste
- 2 tablespoons water
- 1 tablespoon extra-virgin olive oil
- 1 bunch scallions, sliced
- 1 pound medium shrimp, peeled and deveined
- 1 cup frozen peas
- 1 red bell pepper, diced
- 1 can full-fat coconut milk
- Kosher salt

Directions:

1. In a small bowl, whisk together the red curry paste and water. Set aside.
2. Select SEAR/SAUTÉ and set to MED. Select START/STOP to begin. Let preheat for 3 minutes.
3. Add the oil and scallions. Cook for 2 minutes.
4. Add the shrimp, peas, and bell pepper. Stir well to combine. Stir in the red curry paste. Cook for 5 minutes, until the peas are tender.
5. Stir in coconut milk and cook for an additional 5 minutes until shrimp is cooked through and the bisque is thoroughly heated.
6. Season with salt and serve immediately.

Nutrition Info:

- Calories: 460,Total Fat: 32g,Sodium: 902mg,Carbohydrates: 16g,Protein: 29g.

Vegan & Vegetable

Mushroom Poutine 44

Veggie Lasagna.................44

Zucchini Quinoa Stuffed Red Peppers.....................45

Italian Sausage With Garlic Mash 45

Beets And Carrots.............45

Carrots Walnuts Salad 46

Pineapple Appetizer Ribs .46

Cheesy Corn Casserole.....46

Crème De La Broc............46

Rustic Veggie Tart 47

Tasty Acorn Squash 47

Vegan Stuffed Peppers.....48

Leeks And Carrots 48

Parsley Mashed Cauliflower 48

Green Minestrone 48

Italian Baked Zucchini 49

Burrito Bowls 49

Aloo Gobi With Cilantro ..50

Vegetarian Stir Fry...........50

Eggplant & Penne Pot 50

Hearty Veggie Soup..........51

Spinach, Tomatoes, And Butternut Squash Stew 51

Pesto With Cheesy Bread .51

Crispy Kale Chips 52

Whole Roasted Broccoli And White Beans With Harissa, Tahini, And Lemon...........52

Baby Porcupine Meatballs 53

Chorizo Mac And Cheese .53

Stuffed Manicotti..............53

Paneer Cutlet 53

Stir Fried Cabbage............54

Rosemary Sweet Potato Medallions 54

Green Squash Gruyere......54

VEGAN & VEGETABLE

Mushroom Poutine

Servings:4
Cooking Time: 46 Minutes

Ingredients:
- 2 tablespoons unsalted butter
- 1 small yellow onion, diced
- 1 garlic clove, minced
- 8 ounces cremini mushrooms, sliced
- ¼ cup red wine
- 3 cups vegetable stock
- ¼ cup all-purpose flour
- Kosher salt
- Freshly ground black pepper
- 1 pound frozen French fries
- 8 ounces Cheddar cheese, cubed

Directions:
1. Select SEAR/SAUTÉ and set to MED. Select START/STOP to begin. Let preheat for 3 minutes.
2. Add the butter, onion, and garlic. Cook, stirring occasionally, for 5 minutes. Add the mushrooms and sauté for 5 minutes. Add the wine and let it simmer and reduce for 3 minutes.
3. In large bowl, slowly whisk together the stock and flour. Whisk this mixture into the vegetables in the pot. Cook the gravy for 10 minutes. Season with salt and pepper. Transfer the gravy to a medium bowl and set aside. Clean out the pot and return to unit.
4. Insert Cook & Crisp Basket and add the French fries. Close crisping lid.
5. Select AIR CRISP, set temperature to 360°F, and set time to 18 minutes. Select START/STOP to begin.
6. Every 5 minutes, open lid and remove and shake basket to ensure even cooking.
7. Once cooking is complete, remove fries from basket and place in the pot. Add the cheese and stir. Cover with the gravy. Close crisping lid.
8. Select AIR CRISP, set temperature to 375°F, and set time 5 minutes. Select START/STOP to begin.
9. When cooking is complete, serve immediately.

Nutrition Info:
- Calories: 550,Total Fat: 32g,Sodium: 941mg,Carbohydrates: 42g,Protein: 20g.

Veggie Lasagna

Servings: 4
Cooking Time: 35 Minutes

Ingredients:
- Nonstick cooking spray
- 2 Portobello mushrooms, sliced ¼-inch thick
- 1 eggplant, cut lengthwise in 6 slices
- 1 yellow squash, cut lengthwise in 4 slices
- 1 red bell pepper, cut in ½-inch strips
- ½ tsp garlic powder
- ½ tsp salt
- ½ tsp black pepper
- ½ cup ricotta cheese, fat free, divided
- 2 tbsp. fresh basil, chopped, divided
- ¾ cup mozzarella cheese, grated fine, divided
- ¼ cup tomato sauce

Directions:
1. Spray the cooking pot and rack with cooking spray.
2. Place a single layer of vegetables in the cooking pot. Add the rack and place remaining vegetables on it. Season vegetables with garlic powder, salt, and pepper.
3. Add the tender-crisp lid and set to roast on 425°F. Cook vegetables 15-20 minutes until tender, stirring halfway through cooking time. Transfer to a large plate.
4. Spray an 8x8-inch baking pan with cooking spray.
5. Line the bottom of the pan with 3 slices of eggplant. Spread ¼ cup ricotta cheese, 1 tablespoon basil, and ¼ cup mozzarella over eggplant.
6. Layer with remaining vegetables, then remaining ricotta, basil and ¼ cup mozzarella on top. End with 3 slices of eggplant and pour tomato sauce over then sprinkle remaining cheese over the top.
7. Add the rack back to the cooking pot and place the lasagna on it. Add the tender-crisp lid and set to bake on 350°F. Bake 15-20 minutes until cheese is melted and lasagna is heated through, serve.

Nutrition Info:
- Calories 145,Total Fat 3g,Total Carbs 18g,Protein 14g,Sodium 490mg.

Zucchini Quinoa Stuffed Red Peppers

Servings: 4
Cooking Time: 40 Min

Ingredients:
- 1 small zucchini; chopped
- 4 red bell peppers
- 2 large tomatoes; chopped
- 1 small onion; chopped
- 2 cloves garlic, minced
- 1 cup quinoa, rinsed /130g
- 1 cup grated Gouda cheese /130g
- ½ cup chopped mushrooms /65g
- 1 ½ cup water /375ml
- 2 cups chicken broth /500ml
- 1 tbsp olive oil /15ml
- ½ tsp smoked paprika /2.5g
- Salt and black pepper to taste

Directions:
1. Select Sear/Sauté mode on High. Once it is ready, add the olive oil to heat and then add the onion and garlic. Sauté for 3 minutes to soften, stirring occasionally.
2. Include the tomatoes, cook for 3 minutes and then add the quinoa, zucchinis, and mushrooms. Season with paprika, salt, and black pepper and stir with a spoon. Cook for 5 to 7 minutes, then, turn the pot off.
3. Use a knife to cut the bell peppers in halves (lengthwise) and remove their seeds and stems.
4. Spoon the quinoa mixture into the bell peppers. Put the peppers in a greased baking dish and pour the broth over.
5. Wipe the pot clean with some paper towels, and pour the water into it. After, fit the steamer rack at the bottom of the pot.
6. Place the baking dish on top of the reversible rack, cover with aluminum foil, close the lid, secure the pressure valve, and select Pressure mode on High pressure for 15 minutes. Press Start/Stop.
7. Once the timer has ended, do a quick pressure release and open the lid. Remove the aluminum foil and sprinkle with the gouda cheese.
8. Close the crisping lid, select Bake/Roast mode and cook for 10 minutes on 375 °F or 191°C. Arrange the stuffed peppers on a serving platter and serve right away or as a side to a meat dish.

Italian Sausage With Garlic Mash

Servings: 6
Cooking Time: 30 Min

Ingredients:
- 6 Italian sausages
- 4 large potatoes, peeled and cut into 1½-inch chunks
- 2 garlic cloves, smashed
- ⅓ cup butter, melted /44ml
- ¼ cup milk; at room temperature, or more as needed /62.5ml
- 1 ½ cups water /375ml
- 1 tbsp olive oil /15ml
- 1 tbsp chopped chives/15g
- salt and ground black pepper to taste

Directions:
1. Select Sear/Sauté, set to Medium High, and choose Start/Stop to preheat the pot and heat olive oil. Cook for 8-10 minutes, turning periodically until browned. Set aside. Wipe the pot with paper towels. Add in water and set the reversible rack over water. Place potatoes onto the reversible rack.
2. Seal the pressure lid, choose Pressure, set to High, and set the timer to 12 minutes. Press Start.
3. When ready, release the pressure quickly. Remove reversible rack from the pot. Drain water from the pot. Return potatoes to pot. Add in salt, butter, pepper, garlic, and milk and use a hand masher to mash until no large lumps remain.
4. Using an immersion blender, blend potatoes on Low for 1 minute until fluffy and light. Avoid over-blending to ensure the potatoes do not become gluey!
5. Transfer the mash to a serving plate, top with sausages and scatter chopped chives over to serve.

Beets And Carrots

Servings: 4
Cooking Time: 20 Minutes

Ingredients:
- 1-pound beets, peeled and roughly cubed
- 1-pound baby carrots, peeled
- Black pepper and salt to the taste
- 2 tablespoons olive oil
- 1 tablespoon chives, minced

Directions:
1. In a suitable, mix the beets with the carrots and the other ingredients and toss.
2. Put the beets and carrots in the Foodi's basket.

3. Cook on Air Crisp at 390 °F for 20 minutes, divide between plates and serve.

Nutrition Info:
• Calories: 150; Fat: 4.5g; Carbohydrates: 7.3g; Protein: 3.6g

Carrots Walnuts Salad

Servings: 4
Cooking Time: 15 Minutes

Ingredients:
• 4 carrots, roughly shredded
• ½ cup walnuts, sliced
• 3 tablespoons balsamic vinegar
• 1 cup chicken stock
• Black pepper and salt to the taste
• 1 tablespoon olive oil

Directions:
1. In your Ninja Foodi, mix the carrots with the vinegar and the other ingredients except for the walnuts.
2. Put the pressure cooking lid on and cook on High for 15 minutes.
3. Release the pressure quickly for 5 minutes, divide the mix between plates and serve with the walnuts sprinkled on top.

Nutrition Info:
• Calories: 120; Fat: 4.5g; Carbohydrates: 5.3g; Protein: 1.3g

Pineapple Appetizer Ribs

Servings: 4
Cooking Time: 30 Min

Ingredients:
• 2 lb. cut spareribs /900g
• 2 cups water /500ml
• 5 oz. canned pineapple juice /150ml
• 7 oz. salad dressing /210g
• Garlic salt
• Salt and black pepper

Directions:
1. Sprinkle the ribs with salt and pepper and place them in a saucepan. Pour water and cook the ribs for around 12 minutes on high heat. Drain the ribs and arrange them in the Ninja Foodi.
2. Sprinkle with garlic salt. Close the crisping lid and cook for 15 minutes at 390 °F or 199°Con Air Crisp mode.

3. Meanwhile, prepare the sauce by combining the salad dressing and the pineapple juice. Serve the ribs with this delicious dressing sauce!

Cheesy Corn Casserole

Servings: 6
Cooking Time: 4 Hours

Ingredients:
• Nonstick cooking spray
• 1 ¾ lbs. corn
• 8 oz. cream cheese, cubed
• 1 cup cheddar cheese, grated
• ¼ cup butter, sliced
• ¼ cup heavy cream
• ½ tsp salt
• ¼ tsp pepper

Directions:
1. Spray the cooking pot with cooking spray.
2. Add all the ingredients to the cooking pot and stir to mix.
3. Add the lid and set to slow cook on low. Cook 3 ½ - 4 hours, stirring occasionally, until all the cheese has melted and casserole is hot. Stir well before serving.

Nutrition Info:
• Calories 420,Total Fat 31g,Total Carbs 29g,Protein 12g,Sodium 540mg.

Crème De La Broc

Servings: 6
Cooking Time: 25 Min

Ingredients:
• 1 ½ cups grated yellow and white Cheddar cheese + extra for topping /195g
• 1 ½ oz. cream cheese /195g
• 1 medium Red onion; chopped
• 3 cloves garlic, minced
• 4 cups chopped broccoli florets, only the bushy tops/520g
• 3 cups heavy cream /750ml
• 3 cups vegetable broth /750ml
• 4 tbsp butter /60g
• 4 tbsp flour /60g
• 1 tsp Italian Seasoning /5g
• Salt and black pepper to taste

Directions:
1. Select Sear/Sauté mode, adjust to High and melt the butter once the pot is ready. Add the flour and use

a spoon to stir until it clumps up. Gradually pour in the heavy cream while stirring until white sauce forms. Fetch out the butter sauce into a bowl and set aside.

2. Press Stop and add the onions, garlic, broth, broccoli, Italian seasoning, and cream cheese. Use a wooden spoon to stir the mixture.

3. Seal the lid, and select Pressure mode on High pressure for 12 minutes. Press Start/Stop. Once the timer has ended, do a quick pressure release.

4. Add in butter sauce and cheddar cheese, salt, and pepper. Close the crisping lid and cook on Broil mode for 3 minutes. Dish the soup into serving bowls, top it with extra cheese, to serve.

Rustic Veggie Tart

Servings: 6
Cooking Time: 40 Minutes

Ingredients:

- 1 tbsp. olive oil
- 3 cups cherry tomatoes
- ½ tsp salt, divided
- 1/8 tsp red pepper flakes
- 1 cup fresh corn kernels
- 1 zucchini, chopped
- 5-6 green onions, sliced thin
- 1 ¼ cups flour
- 8 tbsp. butter, sliced
- ¼ cup sour cream
- 2 tsp fresh lemon juice
- ¼ cup ice water
- ½ cup parmesan cheese
- 1 egg yolk
- 1 tsp water

Directions:

1. In a large bowl, combine flour and ¼ tsp salt. Cut in butter until mixture resembles coarse crumbs.

2. In a small bowl, whisk together sour cream, lemon juice, and water until combined. Add to flour mixture and stir until it forms a soft dough. Form dough into a ball and wrap with plastic wrap, refrigerate at least 1 hour.

3. Add oil to the cooking pot and set to sauté on med-high heat.

4. Add tomatoes, remaining salt, and red pepper flakes, cover and cook until tomatoes burst, turning tomatoes frequently.

5. Reduce heat to medium and add zucchini. Cook 2 minutes until they soften. Add corn and cook 1 minute

more. Stir in scallions and turn off the heat. Transfer to a large plate and let cool.

6. Wipe out the cooking pot and add the rack.

7. On a floured surface, roll out dough to a 12-inch circle. Transfer to a piece of parchment paper.

8. Sprinkle vegetables with half the parmesan cheese and spoon into the center of the dough, leaving a 2-inch border. Sprinkle most of the remaining parmesan over the vegetables.

9. Fold edges over the filling, pleating as you go.

10. In a small bowl, beat together egg yolk and teaspoon of water. Brush the crust with egg yolk glaze and sprinkle with the last of the parmesan.

11. Carefully pick up the parchment paper and transfer to the rack in the cooking pot. Add the tender-crisp lid and set to bake on 400°F. Bake 30-40 minutes until golden brown. Transfer to wire rack to cool 5 minutes before serving.

Nutrition Info:

- Calories 159, Total Fat 10g, Total Carbs 14g, Protein 4g, Sodium 170mg.

Tasty Acorn Squash

Servings: 4
Cooking Time: 30 Min

Ingredients:

- 1 lb. acorn squash, peeled and cut into chunks /450g
- ½ cup water /125ml
- 2 tbsp butter /30g
- 1 tbsp dark brown sugar /15g
- 1 tbsp cinnamon /15g
- 3 tbsp honey; divided 45ml
- salt and ground black pepper to taste

Directions:

1. In a small bowl, mix 1 tbsp honey and water; pour into the pressure cooker's pot. Add in squash. Seal the and cook on High pressure for 4 minutes. Press Start. When ready, release the pressure quickly.

2. Transfer the squash to a serving dish. Turn Foodi to Sear/Sauté.

3. Mix brown sugar, cinnamon, the remaining 2 tbsp honey and the liquid in the pot; cook as you stir for 4 minutes to obtain a thick consistency and starts to turn caramelized and golden. Spread honey glaze over squash; add pepper and salt for seasoning.

Vegan Stuffed Peppers

Servings: 4
Cooking Time: 35 Minutes

Ingredients:
- Nonstick cooking spray
- 2 bell peppers, halved lengthwise & cleaned
- 2 tbsp. olive oil
- ½ cup onion, chopped
- 4 cloves garlic, chopped fine
- 2 tomatoes, chopped fine
- ¼ tsp salt
- ¼ cup fresh parsley, chopped
- 1/3 cup dry bread crumbs
- 2 tbsp. dry white wine
- ¼ tsp pepper
- 2 tbsp. parmesan cheese

Directions:
1. Spray an 8x8-inch baking dish with cooking spray.
2. Fill the cooking pot halfway full with water. Set to sauté on high heat and bring to a boil.
3. Add the pepper halves and boil 4-5 minutes or until they start to soften. Drain and place peppers in cold water. Drain again.
4. Add oil to the cooking pot and set to medium heat. Add onion and garlic and cook just until onion has softened. Turn off heat and stir in remaining ingredients, except pepper and parmesan cheese, mix well.
5. Spoon the onion mixture into the peppers and place them in prepared dish. Sprinkle with parmesan cheese.
6. Place the rack in the cooking pot and add the peppers. Add the tender-crisp lid and set to bake on 350°F. Bake 35-40 minutes until filling is hot and peppers are tender. Serve immediately.

Nutrition Info:
- Calories 152, Total Fat 8g, Total Carbs 17g, Protein 4g, Sodium 285mg.

Leeks And Carrots

Servings: 4
Cooking Time: 15 Minutes

Ingredients:
- 2 leeks, roughly sliced
- 2 carrots, sliced
- 1 teaspoon ginger powder
- 1 teaspoon garlic powder
- ½ cup chicken stock
- Black pepper and salt to the taste
- 2 tablespoons lemon juice
- 2 tablespoons olive oil
- ½ tablespoon balsamic vinegar

Directions:
1. In your Ninja Foodi, combine the leeks with the carrots and the other ingredients.
2. Put the Ninja Foodi's lid on and cook on High for 15 minutes.
3. Release the pressure quickly for 5 minutes, divide the mix between plates and serve.

Nutrition Info:
- Calories: 133; Fat: 3.4g; Carbohydrates: 5g; Protein: 2.1g

Parsley Mashed Cauliflower

Servings: 4
Cooking Time: 15 Min

Ingredients:
- 1 head cauliflower
- 1/4 cup heavy cream /62.5g
- 2 cups water /500ml
- 1 tbsp fresh parsley, finely chopped /15g
- 1 tbsp butter /15g
- ¼ tsp celery salt /1.25g
- ⅛ tsp freshly ground black pepper /0.625g

Directions:
1. Into the pot, add water and set trivet on top and lay cauliflower head onto the trivet. Seal the pressure lid, choose Pressure, set to High, and set the timer to 8 minutes. Press Start.
2. When ready, release the pressure quickly. Remove the trivet and drain liquid from the pot before returning to the base.
3. Take back the cauliflower to the pot alongside the pepper, heavy cream, salt and butter; use an immersion blender to blend until smooth. Top with parsley and serve.

Green Minestrone

Servings: 4
Cooking Time: 30 Min

Ingredients:
- 1 head broccoli, cut into florets
- 1 zucchini; chopped
- 2 cups chopped kale /260g
- 1 cup green beans /130g
- 2 cups vegetable broth /260g

- 4 celery stalks; sliced thinly
- 1 leek; sliced thinly
- 3 whole black peppercorns
- 2 tbsp olive oil /30ml
- water to cover
- salt to taste

Directions:

1. Into the pressure cooker, add broccoli, leek, green beans, salt, peppercorns, zucchini, and celery. Mix in vegetable broth, oil, and water.

2. Seal the pressure lid, choose Pressure, set to High, and set the timer to 4 minutes. Press Start.

3. Release pressure naturally for 5 minutes, then release the remaining pressure quickly. Add kale into the soup and stir; set to Keep Warm and cook until tender.

Italian Baked Zucchini

Servings: 6
Cooking Time: 45 Minutes

Ingredients:

- Nonstick cooking spray
- 2 tsp olive oil
- 2 lbs. zucchini, sliced ¼-inch thick
- ¼ cup onion, chopped
- 3 plum tomatoes, cut in ½- inch pieces
- 1 tbsp. parmesan cheese
- ½ cup Italian blend cheese, grated
- 1 tsp garlic powder
- 1 tsp Italian seasoning
- ¼ tsp pepper
- 1 tbsp. Italian bread crumbs

Directions:

1. Spray the cooking pot with cooking spray.

2. Add the oil to the cooking pot and set to sauté on med-high heat.

3. Add the zucchini and onion and cook, stirring occasionally, 5 minutes, until softened.

4. Stir in tomatoes, parmesan, Italian blend cheese, garlic powder, Italian seasonings, and pepper. Cook 3 minutes, stirring occasionally. Sprinkle bread crumbs over the top.

5. Add the tender-crisp lid and set to bake on 375°F. Bake 25-30 minutes until golden brown. Serve.

Nutrition Info:

- Calories 91,Total Fat 4g,Total Carbs 8g,Protein 7g,-Sodium 146mg.

Burrito Bowls

Servings: 4
Cooking Time: 30 Min

Ingredients:

- 1 can diced tomatoes /435g
- 1 can black beans, drained and rinsed /435g
- 1 ½ cups vegetable stock /375ml
- 1 cup frozen corn kernels /130g
- 1 cup quinoa, rinsed /130g
- 1 avocado; sliced
- 1 onion
- 2 garlic cloves, minced
- 2 tbsp chopped cilantro /30g
- 1 tbsp roughly chopped fresh coriander /15g
- 2 tbsp olive oil /30ml
- 1 tbsp chili powder /15g
- 2 tsp ground cumin /10g
- 2 tsp paprika /10g
- 1 tsp salt /5g
- ½ tsp black pepper /2.5g
- ¼ tsp cayenne pepper /1.25g
- Cheddar cheese, grated for garnish

Directions:

1. Warm oil on Sear/Sauté. Add in onion and cook for 3 to 5 minutes until fragrant. Add garlic and cook for 2 more minutes until soft and golden brown. Add in chili powder, paprika, cayenne pepper, salt, cumin, and black pepper and cook for 1 minute until spices are soft.

2. Pour quinoa into onion and spice mixture and stir to coat quinoa completely in spices. Add diced tomatoes, black beans, vegetable stock, and corn; stir to combine.

3. Seal the pressure lid, choose Pressure, set to High, and set the timer to 7 minutes. Press Start. When ready, release the pressure quickly. Open the lid and let sit for 6 minutes until flavors combine. Use a fork to fluff quinoa and season with pepper and salt if desired.

4. Into quinoa and beans mixture, stir in cilantro and divide among plates. Top with cheese and avocado slices.

Aloo Gobi With Cilantro

Servings: 4
Cooking Time: 40 Min

Ingredients:
- 1 head cauliflower, cored and cut into florets
- 1 potato, peeled and diced
- 4 garlic cloves, minced
- 1 tomato, cored and chopped
- 1 jalapeño pepper, deseeded and minced
- 1 onion, minced
- 1 cup water /250ml
- 1 tbsp curry paste /15g
- 1 tbsp vegetable oil /15ml
- 1 tbsp ghee /15g
- 2 tsp cumin seeds /10g
- 1 tsp ground turmeric /5g
- ½ tsp chili pepper /2.5g
- salt to taste
- A handful of cilantro leaves; chopped

Directions:
1. Warm oil on Sear/Sauté. Add in potato and cauliflower and cook for 8 to 10 minutes until lightly browned; add salt for seasoning. Set the vegetables to a bowl.
2. Add ghee to the pot. Mix in cumin seeds and cook for 10 seconds until they start to pop; add onion and cook for 3 minutes until softened. Mix in garlic; cook for seconds.
3. Add in tomato, curry paste, chili pepper, jalapeño pepper, curry paste, and turmeric; cook for 3 to 5 minutes until the tomato starts to break down.
4. Return potato and cauliflower to the pot. Add water over the vegetables, add more salt if need be, and stir. Seal the pressure lid, choose Pressure, set to High, and set the timer to 4 minutes. Press Start. Release pressure naturally. Top with cilantro and serve.

Vegetarian Stir Fry

Servings: 6
Cooking Time: 10 Minutes

Ingredients:
- 4 cloves garlic, chopped fine
- 2 tbsp. blue agave
- 1 tbsp. light soy sauce
- ¼ tsp ginger
- 1 tbsp. cornstarch
- 1 tsp sesame seeds
- 2 tsp olive oil
- 2 cups fresh broccoli florets
- ¼ lb. fresh snow peas, trimmed
- 1 red bell pepper, cut in ¼-inch strips
- 1 onion, cut in wedges

Directions:
1. In a small bowl, whisk together garlic, agave, soy sauce, ginger, and cornstarch until combined.
2. Set cooker to sauté on medium heat. Add sesame seeds and toast, stirring frequently, 2-3 minutes. Transfer to a plate.
3. Add the oil and increase the heat to med-high. Add broccoli, peas, bell pepper, and onion. Cook until tender-crisp, stirring occasionally, about 4-5 minutes.
4. Stir in the agave mixture and cook 2 minutes until sauce thicken. Serve immediately.

Nutrition Info:
- Calories 58,Total Fat 2g,Total Carbs 8g,Protein 2g,Sodium 98mg.

Eggplant & Penne Pot

Servings: 4
Cooking Time: 20 Minutes

Ingredients:
- 2 tbsp. olive oil
- 1 onion, chopped
- 1 clove garlic, chopped fine
- 1 eggplant, cut in ¼-inch pieces
- 1 red bell pepper, chopped
- ½ tsp salt
- ½ tsp pepper
- 10 oz. tomato sauce
- 2 tsp sugar
- 1 ½ cups baby spinach
- 20 oz. penne pasta, cooked & drained

Directions:
1. Add oil to the cooking pot and set to sauté on med-high.
2. Add onions and cook 2-3 minutes until they start to soften. Add garlic and cook 1 minute more.
3. Add the eggplant, peppers, salt, and pepper and cook about 5 minutes, stirring occasionally.
4. Stir in the tomato sauce and sugar and simmer 3-4 minutes or until eggplant is tender.
5. Stir in the spinach and cook 2-3 minutes until it wilts and is tender.
6. Stir in pasta and cook just until heated through. Serve immediately.

Nutrition Info:
- Calories 238, Total Fat 3g, Total Carbs 45g, Protein 10g, Sodium 288mg.

Hearty Veggie Soup

Servings: 12
Cooking Time: 15 Minutes

Ingredients:
- 2 cups water
- 3 ½ cups vegetable broth, low sodium
- 15 oz. red kidney beans, drained & rinsed
- 16 oz. cannellini beans, drained & rinsed
- 28 oz. tomatoes, crushed
- 10 oz. spinach, chopped
- 1 onion, chopped
- 10 oz. mixed vegetables, frozen
- 1 tsp garlic powder
- ½ tsp pepper
- 1 cup elbow macaroni

Directions:
1. Set the cooker to sauté on med-high heat.
2. Add all the ingredients, except macaroni, and stir to combine. Bring to a boil.
3. Stir in macaroni. Add the lid and set to pressure cook on high. Set timer for 10 minutes. When timer goes off, use natural release to remove the pressure. Stir well and serve.

Nutrition Info:
- Calories 181, Total Fat 1g, Total Carbs 34g, Protein 10g, Sodium 478mg.

Spinach, Tomatoes, And Butternut Squash Stew

Servings: 6
Cooking Time: 65 Min

Ingredients:
- 2 lb. butternut squash, peeled and cubed /900g
- 1 can sundried tomatoes, undrained /450g
- 2 cans chickpeas, drained /450g
- 1 white onion; diced
- 4 garlic cloves, minced
- 4 cups baby spinach /520g
- 4 cups vegetable broth /1000ml
- 1 tbsp butter /15g
- ½ tsp smoked paprika /2.5g
- 1 tsp coriander powder /5g
- 1½ tsp s cumin powder /7.5g

- ½ tsp salt /2.5g
- ½ tsp freshly ground black pepper /2.5g

Directions:
1. Choose Sear/Sauté, set to Medium High, and the timer to 5 minutes; press Start/Stop to preheat the pot. Combine the butter, onion, and garlic in the pot. Cook, stirring occasionally; for 5 minutes or until soft and fragrant.
2. Add the butternut squash, vegetable broth, tomatoes, chickpeas, cumin, paprika, coriander, salt, and black pepper to the pot. Put the pressure lid together and lock in the Seal position.
3. Choose Pressure, set to High, and set the time to 8 minutes; press Start/Stop.
4. When the timer is done reading, perform a quick pressure release. Stir in the spinach to wilt, adjust the taste with salt and black pepper, and serve warm.

Pesto With Cheesy Bread

Servings: 4
Cooking Time: 60 Min

Ingredients:
- 1 medium red onion; diced
- 1 celery stalk; diced
- 1 large carrot, peeled and diced
- 1 small yellow squash; diced
- 1 can chopped tomatoes /420g
- 1 can cannellini beans, rinsed and drained /810g
- 1 bay leaf
- 1 cup chopped zucchini /130g
- ¼ cup shredded Pecorino Romano cheese /32.5g
- ⅓ cup olive oil based pesto /88ml
- 3 cups water /750ml
- 1 Pecorino Romano rind
- 1 garlic clove, minced
- 4 slices white bread
- 3 tbsps butter; at room temperature /45g
- 3 tbsps ghee /45g
- 1 tsp mixed herbs /5g
- ¼ tsp cayenne pepper /1.25g
- ½ tsp salt /2.5g

Directions:
1. On your Foodi, choose Sear/Sauté, and adjust to Medium to preheat the inner pot. Press Start. Add the ghee to the pot to melt and sauté the onion, celery, and carrot for 3 minutes or until the vegetables start to soften.
2. Stir in the yellow squash, tomatoes, beans, water,

zucchini, bay leaf, mixed herbs, cayenne pepper, salt, and Pecorino Romano rind.

3. Seal the pressure lid, choose Pressure, adjust to High, and set the time to 4 minutes. Press Start. In a bowl, mix the butter, shredded cheese, and garlic. Spread the mixture on the bread slices.

4. After cooking the soup, perform a natural pressure release for 2 minutes, then a quick pressure release and carefully open the lid.

5. Adjust the taste of the soup with salt and black pepper, and remove the bay leaf. Put the reversible rack in the upper position of the pot and lay the bread slices in the rack with the buttered-side up.

6. Close the crisping lid. Choose Broil; adjust the cook time to 5 minutes, and Press Start/Stop to begin broiling.

7. When the bread is crispy, carefully remove the rack, and set aside. Ladle the soup into serving bowls and drizzle the pesto over. Serve with the garlic toasts.

Crispy Kale Chips

Servings: 2
Cooking Time: 9 Min

Ingredients:
- 4 cups kale, stemmed and packed /520g
- 1 tbsp of yeast flakes /15g
- 2 tbsp of olive oil /30ml
- 1 tsp of vegan seasoning /5g
- Salt to taste

Directions:
1. In a bowl, add the oil, the kale, the vegan seasoning, and the yeast and mix well. Dump the coated kale in the Ninja Foodi's basket.
2. Set the heat to 370°F or 188°C, close the crisping lid and fry for a total of 6 minutes on Air Crisp mode. Shake it from time to time.

Whole Roasted Broccoli And White Beans With Harissa, Tahini, And Lemon

Servings:4
Cooking Time: 30 Minutes

Ingredients:
- 2 cups water
- 2 small heads broccoli, cut in half
- 2 tablespoons unsalted butter
- ½ white onion, minced
- 2 garlic cloves, minced
- 1 can cannellini beans, rinsed and drained
- 1 can fire-roasted tomatoes and peppers
- 1 tablespoon spicy harissa
- Sea salt
- Freshly ground black pepper
- ¼ cup tahini
- ¼ cup walnuts, toasted and chopped
- Zest of 1 lemon
- Juice of 1 lemon

Directions:
1. Place Reversible Rack in pot, making sure it is in the lowest position. Pour the water into the pot and place the broccoli on the rack. Assemble the pressure lid, making sure the pressure release valve is in the SEAL position.
2. Select STEAM. Set time to 8 minutes. Select START/STOP to begin.
3. When steaming is complete, quick release the pressure by turning the pressure release valve to the VENT position. Carefully remove lid when unit has finished releasing pressure.
4. Remove rack and broccoli and set aside. Drain the remaining water from the pot and reinsert it in base.
5. Select SEAR/SAUTÉ and set to HI. Select START/STOP to begin. Let preheat for 5 minutes.
6. Add the butter to pot. Once melted, add the onions and garlic and cook for 3 minutes. Add the beans, tomatoes, harissa, and season with salt and pepper. Cook for 4 minutes.
7. Reinsert rack and broccoli. Close crisping lid.
8. Select AIR CRISP, set temperature to 390°F, and set time to 15 minutes. Select START/STOP to begin.
9. After 10 minutes, open lid and flip the broccoli. Close lid and continue cooking.
10. When cooking is complete, remove rack with broccoli from pot. Place the beans in serving dishes and top with the broccoli. Drizzle tahini over the broccoli and sprinkle with walnuts. Garnish with the lemon zest and juice and serve.

Nutrition Info:
- Calories: 426,Total Fat: 25g,Sodium: 435mg,Carbohydrates: 39g,Protein: 15g.

Baby Porcupine Meatballs

Servings: 4
Cooking Time: 30 Min

Ingredients:
- 1 lb. of ground beef /450g
- 1 onion; chopped
- 1 green bell pepper, finely chopped
- 1 garlic clove, minced
- 1 cup rice /130g
- 2 cups of tomato juice /500ml
- 2 tbsp Worcestershire sauce /30ml
- 1 tsp celery salt /5g
- 1 tsp oregano /5g

Directions:
1. Combine the rice, ground beef, onion, celery, salt, green peppers, and garlic. Shape into balls of 1 inch each. Arrange the balls in the basket of the Ninja Foodi. Close the crisping lid and cook for 15 minutes at 320°F or 160°C.
2. After 8 minutes, shape the balls. Heat the tomato juice, cloves, oregano, and Worcestershire sauce in a saucepan over medium heat.
3. Pour in the meatballs, bring to a boil, reduce the heat and simmer for 10 minutes, stirring often. Serve warm.

Chorizo Mac And Cheese

Servings: 6
Cooking Time: 30 Min

Ingredients:
- 1 pound macaroni /450g
- 3 ounces chorizo; chopped /90g
- 2 cups milk /500ml
- 2 cups Cheddar cheese, shredded /260g
- 3 cups water /750ml
- 2 tbsp minced garlic /30g
- 1 tbsp garlic powder /15g
- salt to taste

Directions:
1. Put chorizo in the pot of your Foodi, select Sear/Sauté and stir-fry until crisp, about 5 minutes. Press Start. Set aside. Wipe the pot with kitchen paper. Add in water, macaroni, and salt to taste. Seal lid and cook on for 5 minutes High Pressure. Press Start.
2. When ready, release the pressure quickly. Stir in cheese and milk until the cheese melts. Divide the mac and cheese between serving bowls. Top with chorizo and serve.

Stuffed Manicotti

Servings: 4
Cooking Time: 50 Minutes

Ingredients:
- Nonstick cooking spray
- 8 manicotti shells, cooked & drained
- ½ onion, chopped
- 1 cloves garlic, chopped fine
- 1 cup mushrooms, chopped
- 16 oz. ricotta cheese, fat free
- ½ cup mozzarella cheese, grated
- 1 egg
- 1 cup spinach, chopped
- ¾ tsp Italian seasoning
- ¼ tsp pepper
- 1 cups light spaghetti sauce
- 1 tbsp. parmesan cheese, grated

Directions:
1. Spray the cooking pot and an 8x8-inch baking pan with cooking spray.
2. Set cooker to sauté on med-high heat. Add onion and garlic and cook until tender, about 3-4 minutes.
3. Add mushrooms and cook until browned. Turn off the heat.
4. In a large bowl, combine ricotta and mozzarella cheeses, egg, spinach, Italian seasoning, and pepper, mix well.
5. Add the mushroom mixture to the cheese mixture and stir to combine. Spoon into manicotti shells and lay in the prepared pan.
6. Pour the spaghetti sauce over the top and sprinkle with parmesan cheese. Cover with foil.
7. Place the rack in the cooking pot and add the manicotti. Add the tender-crisp lid and set to bake on 400°F. Bake 30-35 minutes or until heated through. Serve immediately.

Nutrition Info:
- Calories 367,Total Fat 19g,Total Carbs 27g,Protein 24g,Sodium 308mg.

Paneer Cutlet

Servings: 1
Cooking Time: 15 Min

Ingredients:
- 1 small onion, finely chopped
- 2 cup grated paneer /260g

- 1 cup grated cheese /130g
- ½ tsp chai masala /2.5g
- 1 tsp butter /5g
- ½ tsp garlic powder /2.5g
- ½ tsp oregano /2.5g
- ½ tsp salt /2.5g

Directions:

1. Preheat the Ninja Foodi to 350 °F or 177°C. Oil the Ninja Foodi basket. Mix all Ingredients in a bowl, until well incorporated.

2. Make cutlets out of the mixture and place them on the greased baking dish. Place the baking dish in the Ninja Foodi and cook the cutlets for 10 minutes.

Stir Fried Cabbage

Servings: 6
Cooking Time: 10 Minutes

Ingredients:

- 1 tbsp. olive oil
- 1 onion, halved & sliced
- 2 carrots, sliced thin
- 3 cloves garlic, chopped fine
- ½ head green cabbage, shredded
- 2 tbsp. soy sauce, low sodium
- ½ tsp ginger
- 1 tbsp. water

Directions:

1. Add oil to the cooking pot and set to sauté on med-high heat.

2. Add the onion, carrots, garlic, and cabbage and cook, stirring frequently, until tender, about 6-8 minutes.

3. Stir in remaining ingredients and cook another 5 minutes until heated through. Serve immediately.

Nutrition Info:

- Calories 44,Total Fat 2g,Total Carbs 5g,Protein 1g,-Sodium 185mg.

Rosemary Sweet Potato Medallions

Servings: 4
Cooking Time: 25 Min

Ingredients:

- 4 sweet potatoes, scrubbed clean and dried
- 1 cup water /250ml
- 2 tbsp butter /30g
- 1 tbsp fresh rosemary /15g
- 1 tsp garlic powder /5g
- salt to taste

Directions:

1. Into the pot, add water and place the reversible rack over the water. Use a fork to prick sweet potatoes all over and set onto the reversible rack.

2. Seal the pressure lid, choose Pressure, set to High, and set the timer to 12 minutes. Press Start. When ready, release the pressure quickly. Transfer sweet potatoes to a cutting board and slice into 1/2-inch medallions and ensure they are peeled.

3. Melt butter in the pressure cooker on Sear/Sauté. Add in the medallions and cook each side for 2 to 3 minutes until browned. Apply salt and garlic powder to season. Serve topped with fresh rosemary.

Green Squash Gruyere

Servings: 4
Cooking Time: 70 Min

Ingredients:

- 1 large green squash; sliced
- 2 cups tomato sauce /500ml
- 1 cup shredded mozzarella cheese /130g
- 1½ cups panko breadcrumbs /195g
- ⅓ cup grated Gruyere cheese /44g
- 3 tbsps melted unsalted butter /45ml
- 2 tsp s salt /10g

Directions:

1. Season the squash slices on both sides with salt and place the slices on a wire rack to drain liquid for 5 to 10 minutes. In a bowl, combine the melted butter, breadcrumbs, and Gruyere cheese and set aside.

2. Rinse the squash slices with water and blot dry with paper towel. After, arrange the squash in the inner pot in a single layer as much as possible and pour the tomato sauce over the slices.

3. Seal the pressure lid, choose Pressure, set to High, and the time to 5 minutes. Press Start to commence cooking. When the timer has read to the end, perform a quick pressure release. Sprinkle the squash slices with the mozzarella cheese.

4. Close the crisping lid. Choose Bake/Roast; adjust the temperature to 375°F or 191°C and the cook time to 2 minutes. Press Start to broil.

5. After, carefully open the lid and sprinkle the squash with the breadcrumb mixture. Close the crisping lid again, choose Bake/Roast, adjust the temperature to 375°F, and the cook time to 8 minutes. Press Start to continue broiling. Serve immediately.

Poultry

Greek Chicken................56
Stuffed Whole Chicken.....56
Honey Garlic Chicken And
Okra........................56
Bacon & Cranberry Stuffed
Turkey Breast 57
Turkey Casserole.............57
Chicken Thighs With
Cabbage......................57
Rosemary Lemon Chicken58
Cheesy Basil Stuffed
Chicken......................58
Chipotle Raspberry Chicken
58
Taiwanese Chicken...........59
Herb Roasted Drumsticks.59
Paprika Chicken.............59
Chicken And Quinoa Soup59
Mini Turkey Loaves.........60
Shredded Buffalo Chicken60
Ginger Orange Chicken
Tenders......................60
Tangy Chicken & Rice.....61

Turkey Breakfast Sausage 61
Chicken With Tomatoes And
Capers......................61
Sour Cream & Cheese
Chicken......................62
Lemon Chicken..............62
Garlic-herb Chicken And
Rice........................62
Turkey Enchilada Casserole
63
Chicken Pot Pie.............63
Chicken Chickpea Chili....64
Tuscan Chicken & Pasta...64
Apricot Bbq Duck Legs....64
Cheesy Chicken &
Mushrooms...................65
Chicken Bruschetta..........65
Bacon Ranch Chicken Bake
65
Buttered Turkey.............66
Chicken With Roasted Red
Pepper Sauce 66

Greek Chicken

Servings: 6
Cooking Time: 45 Min

Ingredients:
- 1 whole chicken; cut in pieces /1350g
- ½ cup olive oil /125ml
- 3 garlic cloves; minced
- Juice from 1 lemon
- ½ cup white wine /125ml
- 1 tbsp chopped fresh oregano /15g
- 1 tbsp fresh thyme /15g
- 1 tbsp fresh rosemary /15g
- Salt and black pepper, to taste

Directions:
1. In a large bowl, combine the garlic, rosemary, thyme, olive oil, lemon juice, oregano, salt, and pepper. Mix all ingredients very well and spread the mixture into the Foodi basket.
2. Stir in the chicken. Sprinkle with wine and cook for 45 minutes on Air Crisp mode at 380 °F or 194°C.

Stuffed Whole Chicken

Servings: 6
Cooking Time: 8 Hours

Ingredients:
- 1 cup mozzarella cheese
- 4 whole garlic cloves, peeled
- 1 whole chicken 2 pounds, cleaned and pat dried
- Black pepper and salt, to taste
- 2 tablespoons fresh lemon juice

Directions:
1. Stuff the chicken cavity with garlic cloves and mozzarella cheese.
2. Season chicken generously with black pepper and salt.
3. Transfer chicken to your Ninja Foodi and drizzle lemon juice.
4. Lock and secure the Ninja Foodi's lid and set to "Slow Cooker" mode, let it cook on LOW for 8 hours.
5. Once done, serve and enjoy.

Nutrition Info:
- Calories: 309; Fat: 12g; Carbohydrates: 1.6g; Pro-

tein: 45g

Honey Garlic Chicken And Okra

Servings: 4
Cooking Time: 25 Min

Ingredients:
- 4 boneless; skinless chicken breasts; sliced
- 4 spring onions, thinly sliced
- 6 garlic cloves, grated
- ⅓ cup honey /84ml
- 1 cup rice, rinsed /130g
- ¼ cup tomato puree /62.5ml
- ½ cup soy sauce /125ml
- 2 cups water /500ml
- 2 cups frozen okra /260g
- 1 tbsp cornstarch /15g
- 2 tbsp rice vinegar /30ml
- 1 tbsp olive oil /15ml
- 1 tbsp water /15ml
- 2 tsp toasted sesame seeds /10g
- ½ tsp salt /2.5g

Directions:
1. In the inner pot of the Foodi, mix garlic, tomato puree, vinegar, soy sauce, ginger, honey, and oil; toss in chicken to coat. In an ovenproof bowl, mix water, salt and rice. Set the reversible rack on top of chicken. Lower the bowl onto the reversible rack.
2. Seal the pressure lid, choose Pressure, set to High, and set the timer to 10 minutes; press Start. Release pressure naturally for 5 minutes, release the remaining pressure quickly.
3. Use a fork to fluff the rice. Lay okra onto the rice. Allow the okra steam in the residual heat for 3 minutes. Take the trivet and bowl from the pot. Set the chicken to a plate.
4. Press Sear/Sauté. In a small bowl, mix 1 tbsp of water and cornstarch until smooth; stir into the sauce and cook for 3 to 4 minutes until thickened.
5. Divide the rice, chicken, and okra between 4 bowls. Drizzle sauce over each portion; garnish with spring onions and sesame seeds.

Bacon & Cranberry Stuffed Turkey Breast

Servings: 4
Cooking Time: 1 Hour

Ingredients:
- ¼ oz. porcini mushrooms, dried
- 1 slice bacon, thick cut, chopped
- ¼ cup shallot, chopped fine
- 2 tbsp. cranberries, dried, chopped
- 1 tsp fresh sage, chopped fine
- ½ cup bread crumbs
- 1 tbsp. fresh parsley, chopped
- 3 tbsp. chicken broth, low sodium
- 2 lb. turkey breast, boneless
- 2 tbsp. butter, soft
- ½ tsp salt

Directions:
1. In a small bowl, add the mushrooms and enough hot water to cover them. Let sit 15 minutes, then drain and chop them.
2. Set the cooker to sauté on medium heat. Add the bacon and cook until crisp. Transfer to a paper-towel lined plate.
3. Add the shallots and cook until they start to brown, about 3-5 minutes. Add the cranberries, sage, and mushrooms and cook, stirring frequently, 2-3 minutes.
4. Stir in bread crumbs, parsley, bacon, and broth and mix well. Transfer to a bowl to cool.
5. Remove the skin from the turkey, in one piece, do not discard. Butterfly the turkey breast and place between 2 sheets of plastic wrap. Pound out to ¼-inch thick.
6. Spread the stuffing over the turkey, leaving a ¾-inch border. Start with a short end and roll up the turkey. Wrap the skin back around the roll.
7. Use butcher string to tie the turkey. Place in the cooking pot and rub with butter. Sprinkle with salt.
8. Add the tender-crisp lid and set to roast on 400°F. Cook 20 minutes, then decrease the heat to 325°F. Cook another 10-15 minutes or until juices run clear. Let rest 10 minutes before slicing and serving.

Nutrition Info:
- Calories 159, Total Fat 7g, Total Carbs 3g, Protein 19g, Sodium 120mg.

Turkey Casserole

Servings: 5
Cooking Time: 45 Min

Ingredients:
- 1 pound turkey breast; cubed /450g
- 2 cans fire-roasted tomatoes /420g
- ½ sweet onion; diced
- 3 cloves garlic; minced
- 1 jalapeno pepper; minced
- 2 bell peppers; cut into thick strips
- 1½ cups water /375ml
- 1 cup salsa /250ml
- 1 tbsp olive oil /15ml
- 5 tbsp fresh oregano; chopped /75g
- 2 tsp ancho chili powder /10g
- 2 tsp chili powder /10g
- 1 tsp ground cumin 5g
- Sea salt to taste

Directions:
1. Warm the oil on Sear/Sauté. Add in garlic, onion and jalapeño and cook for 5 minutes until fragrant. Stir turkey into the pot; cook for 5-6 minutes until browned.
2. Add in salsa, tomatoes, bell peppers, and water; apply a seasoning of sea salt, ancho chili powder, cumin, and chili powder. Seal the pressure lid, choose Pressure, set to High, and set the timer to 10 minutes on High. When ready, release the pressure quickly. Top with oregano and serve.

Chicken Thighs With Cabbage

Servings: 4
Cooking Time: 35 Min

Ingredients:
- 1 pound green cabbage, shredded /450g
- 4 slices pancetta; diced
- 4 chicken thighs, boneless skinless
- 1 cup chicken broth /250ml
- 1 tbsp Dijon mustard/15g
- 1 tbsp lard /15g
- Fresh parsley; chopped
- salt and ground black pepper to taste

Directions:
1. Warm lard on Sear/Sauté. Fry pancetta for 5 minutes until crisp. Set aside. Season chicken with pepper and salt. Sear in Foodi for 2 minutes each side until browned. In a bowl, mix mustard and chicken broth.

2. In your Foodi, add pancetta and chicken broth mixture. Seal the pressure lid, choose Pressure, set to High, and set the timer to 6 minutes. Press Start. When ready, release the pressure quickly.

3. Open the lid, mix in green cabbage, seal again, and cook on High Pressure for 2 minutes. When ready, release the pressure quickly. Serve with sprinkled parsley.

Rosemary Lemon Chicken

Servings: 2
Cooking Time: 60 Min

Ingredients:
- 2 chicken breasts
- 2 rosemary sprigs
- ½ lemon; cut into wedges
- 1 tbsp oyster sauce /15ml
- 3 tbsp brown sugar /45g
- 1 tbsp soy sauce /15ml
- ½ tbsp olive oil /7.5ml
- 1 tsp minced ginger /5g

Directions:
1. Place the ginger, soy sauce, and olive oil, in a bowl. Add the chicken and coat well. Cover the bowl and refrigerate for 30 minutes. Transfer the marinated chicken to the Foodi basket.

2. Close the crisping lid and cook for about 6 minutes on Air Crisp mode at 370 F. or 188°C

3. Mix the oyster sauce, rosemary and brown sugar in a small bowl. Pour the sauce over the chicken. Arrange the lemon wedges in the dish. Return to the Foodi and cook for 13 more minutes on Air Crisp mode.

Cheesy Basil Stuffed Chicken

Servings: 4
Cooking Time: 25 Minutes

Ingredients:
- 4 chicken breasts, boneless & skinless
- 1 tsp garlic powder, divided
- ¼ tsp pepper
- 2 slices Swiss cheese, cut in half
- 12 basil leaves
- 1 tbsp. olive oil
- ¼ cup onion, chopped fine
- ½ cup cherry tomatoes, halved
- 1 tbsp. fresh parsley, chopped
- ½ cup chicken broth, low sodium

Directions:
1. Place chicken between 2 sheets of plastic wrap and pound out to ¼-inch thick.

2. Sprinkle chicken with ½ teaspoon garlic powder and pepper. Place half a slice of cheese on each piece of chicken. Top with 3 basil leaves and roll up, secure with a toothpick.

3. Add oil to the cooking pot and set to sauté on medium heat.

4. Add onion, tomatoes, remaining garlic powder, and parsley. Cook 5 minutes, stirring occasionally.

5. Add broth and cook 1 minute more.

6. Add the chicken to the sauce and turn to coat well, spoon some sauce over the top. Add the tender-crisp lid and set to bake on 350°F. Bake 20-25 minutes until chicken is no longer pink. Serve.

Nutrition Info:
- Calories 215, Total Fat 9g, Total Carbs 2g, Protein 29g, Sodium 175mg.

Chipotle Raspberry Chicken

Servings: 8
Cooking Time: 6 Hours

Ingredients:
- Nonstick cooking spray
- 2 lbs. chicken breasts, boneless & skinless
- 1 cup raspberry preserves, sugar free
- 2 tbsp. chipotle in adobo sauce
- 2 tbsp. fresh lime juice
- ½ tsp cumin

Directions:
1. Spray the cooking pot with cooking spray and add the chicken.

2. In a medium bowl, combine remaining ingredients. Pour over chicken.

3. Add the lid and set to slow cook on low. Cook 6 hours or until chicken is tender. Stir well before serving.

Nutrition Info:
- Calories 168, Total Fat 4g, Total Carbs 8g, Protein 26g, Sodium 144mg.

Taiwanese Chicken

Servings: 4
Cooking Time: 10 Minutes

Ingredients:
- 6 dried red chilis
- ¼ cup sesame oil
- 2 tablespoons ginger
- ¼ cup garlic, minced
- ¼ cup red wine vinegar
- ¼ cup coconut aminos
- Salt, to taste
- 1.2 teaspoon xanthan gum for the finish
- ¼ cup Thai basil, chopped

Directions:
1. Select "Sauté" mode on your Ninja Foodi and add ginger, chilis, garlic and Sauté for 2 minutes.
2. Add remaining ingredients.
3. Lock and secure the Ninja Foodi's lid, then cook on "HIGH" pressure for 10 minutes.
4. Quick-release pressure.
5. Serve and enjoy.

Nutrition Info:
- Calories: 307; Fat: 15g; Carbohydrates: 7g; Protein: 31g

Herb Roasted Drumsticks

Servings: 3
Cooking Time: 40 Minutes

Ingredients:
- Nonstick cooking spray
- 1 tsp paprika
- ¼ tsp salt
- ½ tsp garlic powder
- ¼ tsp onion powder
- ¼ tsp dried thyme
- ¼ tsp pepper
- 6 chicken drumsticks, skin removed, rinsed & patted dry
- ½ tbsp. butter, melted

Directions:
1. Place the rack in the cooking pot and spray it with cooking spray.
2. In a small bowl, combine spices, mix well.
3. Place chicken on the rack and sprinkle evenly over chicken. Drizzle with melted butter.
4. Add the tender-crisp lid and set to roast on 375°F. Bake 35-40 minutes until juices run clear. Serve.

Nutrition Info:
- Calories 319,Total Fat 12g,Total Carbs 0g,Protein 50g,Sodium 505mg.

Paprika Chicken

Servings: 4
Cooking Time: 5 Minutes

Ingredients:
- 4 chicken breasts, skin on
- Black pepper and salt, to taste
- 1 tablespoon olive oil
- ½ cup sweet onion, chopped
- ½ cup heavy whip cream
- 2 teaspoons smoked paprika
- ½ cup sour cream
- 2 tablespoons fresh parsley, chopped

Directions:
1. Season the four chicken breasts with black pepper and salt.
2. Select "Sauté" mode on your Ninja Foodi and add oil; let the oil heat up.
3. Add chicken and sear both sides until properly browned, should take about 15 minutes.
4. Remove chicken and transfer them to a plate.
5. Take a suitable skillet and place it over medium heat; stir in onion.
6. Sauté for 4 minutes until tender.
7. Stir in cream, paprika and bring the liquid to a simmer.
8. Return chicken to the skillet and alongside any juices.
9. Transfer the whole mixture to your Ninja Foodi and lock lid, cook on "HIGH" pressure for 5 minutes.
10. Release pressure naturally over 10 minutes.
11. Stir in sour cream, serve and enjoy.

Nutrition Info:
- Calories: 389; Fat: 30g; Carbohydrates: 4g; Protein: 25g

Chicken And Quinoa Soup

Servings: 6
Cooking Time: 30 Min

Ingredients:
- 2 large boneless; skinless chicken breasts; cubed
- 6 ounces quinoa, rinsed /180g
- 4 ounces mascarpone cheese, at room temperature /120g

- 1 cup milk /250ml
- 1 cup heavy cream /250ml
- 1 cup red onion; chopped /130g
- 1 cup carrots; chopped /130g
- 1 cup celery; chopped /130g
- 4 cups chicken broth 1000ml
- 2 tbsp butter /30g
- 1 tbsp fresh parsley; chopped /15g
- Salt and freshly ground black pepper to taste

Directions:
1. Melt butter on Sear/Sauté. Add carrot, onion, and celery and cook for 5 minutes until tender. Add chicken broth to the pot; mix in parsley, quinoa and chicken. Add pepper and salt for seasoning.
2. Seal the pressure lid, choose Pressure, set to High, and set the timer to 5 minutes. Press Start. When ready, release the pressure quickly. Press Sear/Sauté.
3. Add mascarpone cheese to the soup and stir well to melt completely; mix in heavy cream and milk. Simmer the soup for 3 to 4 minutes until thickened and creamy.

Mini Turkey Loaves

Servings: 6
Cooking Time: 35 Minutes

Ingredients:
- 6 tbsp. barbecue sauce, divided
- 2 tbsp. water
- 2/3 cup oats
- 2 egg whites, lightly beaten
- 2 tsp chili powder
- 2 tsp Worcestershire sauce
- ½ tsp salt
- 1 lb. ground turkey
- 1 onion, chopped fine
- ½ green bell pepper, chopped fine

Directions:
1. Place the rack in the cooking pot and top with a sheet of foil.
2. In a large bowl, combine 3 tablespoons barbecue sauce and water, stir to mix well.
3. Stir in the oats, egg whites, chili powder, Worcestershire, and salt and mix well.
4. Add the turkey, onion, and bell pepper and mix to combine. Form into 6 small oval-shaped loaves and place on the foil.
5. Add the tender-crisp lid and set to bake on 375°F. Bake 30 minutes.

6. Open the lid and spread the remaining barbecue sauce over the tops of the meatloaves. Bake another 5 minutes. Serve.

Nutrition Info:
- Calories 250,Total Fat 11g,Total Carbs 21g,Protein 17g,Sodium 448mg.

Shredded Buffalo Chicken

Servings: 4
Cooking Time: 5 Minutes

Ingredients:
- 2 lbs. chicken breasts, boneless, skinless & cut in 3-inch pieces
- ¾ cup hot pepper sauce
- ½ cup butter
- 1 tbsp. Stevia brown sugar
- 1 tbsp. Worcestershire sauce

Directions:
1. Add all the ingredients to the cooking pot and stir to mix.
2. Add the lid and set to pressure cook on high. Set the timer for 3 minutes. Once the timer goes off, use manual release to remove the pressure.
3. Use an immersion blender to shred the chicken, or transfer mixture to a food processor and pulse until chicken is shredded. Serve.

Nutrition Info:
- Calories 402,Total Fat 27g,Total Carbs 4g,Protein 35g,Sodium 458mg.

Ginger Orange Chicken Tenders

Servings: 4
Cooking Time: 25 Minutes

Ingredients:
- Nonstick cooking spray
- 1 ½ lbs. chicken tenders
- 1 cup orange juice
- 2 tsp tamari, low sodium
- ½ tsp ginger
- 11 oz. mandarin oranges, drained

Directions:
1. Spray the fryer basket with cooking spray.
2. Place chicken in a single layer in the basket, these may need to be cooked in batches.
3. Add the tender-crisp lid and set to air fry on 350°F. Cook 10 minutes, turning over halfway through cook-

ing time.

4. Add all the tenders to the cooking pot.

5. In a small bowl, whisk together orange juice, soy sauce, and ginger. Pour over chicken and stir to coat all the pieces.

6. Set to sauté on medium heat. Cover and cook chicken, stirring occasionally, about 10 minutes.

7. Add the orange slices and cook another 5 minutes. Serve.

Nutrition Info:

• Calories 259,Total Fat 5g,Total Carbs 17g,Protein 36g,Sodium 210mg.

Tangy Chicken & Rice

Servings: 6
Cooking Time: 30 Minutes

Ingredients:

• 3 tsp chili powder
• 1 tsp paprika
• 1 tsp garlic powder
• 1 tsp onion powder
• ¼ tsp cayenne pepper
• 1 tsp salt
• ¼ tsp pepper
• 6 chicken thighs, boneless & skinless
• 2 tbsp. olive oil
• 1 cup rice, uncooked
• 2 ¼ cups chicken broth, low sodium
• 1 tbsp. + 2 tsp fresh lime juice
• 2 tbsp. cilantro, chopped

Directions:

1. In a small bowl, combine the spices and seasonings, mix well. Use half the mixture to season the chicken on both sides.

2. Add the oil to the pot and set to sauté on medium heat. Cook chicken until browned, about 3-4 minutes per side. Transfer to a plate.

3. Add rice, the remaining seasoning mixture, broth, and 1 tablespoon lime juice to the pot, mix well. Place the chicken on top of the rice.

4. Add the lid and cook 20-25 minutes until chicken is cooked through and the liquid is absorbed.

5. Transfer chicken to serving plates. Fluff the rice with a fork, top with cilantro and remaining lime juice. Serve immediately.

Nutrition Info:

• Calories 327,Total Fat 13g,Total Carbs 29g,Protein 23g,Sodium 1168mg.

Turkey Breakfast Sausage

Servings: 8
Cooking Time: 10 Minutes

Ingredients:

• Nonstick cooking spray
• 1 lb. ground turkey
• ½ tsp sage
• ½ tsp marjoram
• ¾ tsp thyme
• ¼ tsp cayenne pepper
• ¼ tsp allspice
• ¼ tsp black pepper
• ¾ tsp salt
• 1 clove garlic, chopped fine
• ¼ cup maple syrup

Directions:

1. Spray the fryer basket with cooking spray and place in the cooking pot.

2. In a large bowl, mix all ingredients until combined. Form into 8 patties.

3. Place the sausage patties in the fryer basket in a single layer. Add the tender-crisp lid and set to air fry on 375°F. Cook about 10 minutes until browned on the outside and cooked through, turning over halfway through cooking time. Serve.

Nutrition Info:

• Calories 126,Total Fat 7g,Total Carbs 7g,Protein 11g,Sodium 252mg.

Chicken With Tomatoes And Capers

Servings: 4
Cooking Time: 45 Min

Ingredients:

• 4 chicken legs
• 1 onion; diced
• 2 garlic cloves; minced
• ⅓ cup red wine /84ml
• 2 cups diced tomatoes /260g
• ⅓ cup capers /44g
• ¼ cup fresh basil /32.5g
• 2 pickles; chopped
• 2 tbsp olive oil /30ml
• sea salt and fresh ground black pepper to taste

Directions:

1. Sprinkle pepper and salt over the chicken. Warm oil on Sear/Sauté. Add in onion and cook for 3 minutes until fragrant; add in garlic and cook for 30 seconds

until softened.

2. Mix the chicken with vegetables and cook for 6 to 7 minutes until lightly browned.

3. Add red wine to the pan to deglaze, scrape the pan's bottom to get rid of any browned bits of food; stir in tomatoes. Seal the pressure lid, choose Pressure, set to High, and set the timer to 12 minutes; press Start.

4. When ready, release the pressure quickly. To the chicken mixture, add basil, capers and pickles. Serve the chicken in plates covered with the tomato sauce mixture.

Sour Cream & Cheese Chicken

Servings: 8
Cooking Time: 25 Minutes

Ingredients:
- Nonstick cooking spray
- 1 cup sour cream
- 2 tsp garlic powder
- 1 tsp seasoned salt
- ½ tsp pepper
- 1 ½ cups parmesan cheese, divided
- 3 lbs. chicken breasts, boneless

Directions:
1. Spray the cooking pot with cooking spray.
2. In a medium bowl, combine sour cream, garlic powder, seasoned salt, pepper, and 1 cup parmesan cheese, mix well.
3. Place the chicken in the cooking pot. Spread the sour cream mixture over the top and sprinkle with remaining parmesan cheese.
4. Add the tender-crisp lid and set to bake on 375°F. Bake chicken 25-30 minutes until cooked through.
5. Set cooker to broil and cook another 2-3 minutes until top is lightly browned. Serve immediately.

Nutrition Info:
- Calories 377,Total Fat 21g,Total Carbs 3g,Protein 41g,Sodium 737mg.

Lemon Chicken

Servings: 4
Cooking Time: 18 Minutes

Ingredients:
- 4 bone-in, skin-on chicken thighs
- Black pepper and salt to taste
- 2 tablespoons butter
- 2 teaspoons garlic, minced

- ½ cup herbed chicken stock
- ½ cup heavy whip cream
- ½ a lemon, juiced

Directions:
1. Season the four chicken thighs generously with black pepper and salt.
2. Set your Ninja Foodi to sauté mode and add oil, let it heat up.
3. Add thigh, Sauté on both sides for 6 minutes.
4. Remove thigh to a platter and keep it on the side.
5. Add garlic, cook for 2 minutes.
6. Whisk in chicken stock, heavy cream, lemon juice and gently stir.
7. Bring the mix to a simmer and reintroduce chicken.
8. Lock and secure the Ninja Foodi's lid and cook for 10 minutes on "HIGH" pressure.
9. Release pressure over 10 minutes.
10. Serve and enjoy.

Nutrition Info:
- Calories: 294; Fat: 26g; Carbohydrates: 4g; Protein: 12g

Garlic-herb Chicken And Rice

Servings:4
Cooking Time: 14 Minutes

Ingredients:
- 1 box rice pilaf
- 1¾ cups water
- 1 tablespoon unsalted butter
- 4 boneless, skin-on chicken thighs
- 1 tablespoon extra-virgin olive oil
- 1 teaspoon kosher salt
- 1 teaspoon garlic powder

Directions:
1. Place the rice pilaf, water, and butter in the pot and stir.
2. Place Reversible Rack in pot, making sure it is in the higher position. Place the chicken thighs on the rack. Assemble pressure lid, making sure the pressure release valve is in the SEAL position.
3. Select PRESSURE and set to HI. Set time to 4 minutes. Select START/STOP to begin.
4. Stir together the olive oil, salt, and garlic powder in a small bowl.
5. When pressure cooking is complete, quick release the pressure by moving the pressure release valve to the VENT position. Carefully remove lid when unit has finished releasing pressure.

6. Brush the chicken with the olive oil mixture. Close crisping lid.

7. Select BROIL and set time to 10 minutes. Select START/STOP to begin.

8. When cooking is complete, serve the chicken with the rice.

Nutrition Info:

• Calories: 451,Total Fat: 32g,Sodium: 577mg,Carbohydrates: 18g,Protein: 23g.

Turkey Enchilada Casserole

Servings: 6
Cooking Time: 70 Min

Ingredients:

• 1 pound boneless; skinless turkey breasts /450g
• 2 cups shredded Monterey Jack cheese; divided /260g
• 2 cups enchilada sauce /500ml
• 1 yellow onion; diced
• 2 garlic cloves; minced
• 1 can pinto beans, drained and rinsed /450g
• 1 bag frozen corn /480g
• 8 tortillas, each cut into 8 pieces
• 1 tbsp butter /15g
• ¼ tsp salt /1.25g
• ¼ tsp freshly ground black pepper /1.25g

Directions:

1. Choose Sear/Sauté on the pot and set to Medium High. Choose Start/Stop to preheat the pot. Melt the butter and cook the onion for 3 minutes, stirring occasionally. Stir in the garlic and cook until fragrant, about 1 minute more.

2. Put the turkey and enchilada sauce in the pot, and season with salt and black pepper. Stir to combine. Seal the pressure lid, choose Pressure, set to High, and set the time to 15 minutes. Choose Start/Stop.

3. When done cooking, perform a quick pressure release and carefully open the lid. Shred the turkey with two long forks while being careful not to burn your hands. Mix in the pinto beans, tortilla pieces, corn, and half of the cheese to the pot. Sprinkle the remaining cheese evenly on top of the casserole.

4. Close the crisping lid. Choose Broil and set the time to 5 minutes. Press Start/Stop to begin broiling. When ready, allow the casserole to sit for 5 minutes before serving.

Chicken Pot Pie

Servings: 8
Cooking Time: 25 Minutes

Ingredients:

• Nonstick cooking spray
• 1 tbsp. light butter
• ½ cup onion, chopped
• 8 oz. mushrooms, chopped
• 1 ½ cup frozen mixed vegetables, thawed
• 3 cups chicken, cooked & chopped
• ½ tsp thyme
• ½ tsp salt
• ¼ tsp pepper
• 1 cup chicken broth, low sodium
• ½ cup evaporated milk, fat free
• 2 tbsp. flour
• 4 slices refrigerated crescent rolls, low fat

Directions:

1. Spray an 8-inch deep dish pie plate with cooking spray.

2. Add the butter to the cooking pot and set to sauté on med-high to melt.

3. Add onions and mushrooms and cook 3-5 minutes until they start to soften. Add vegetables, chicken, thyme, salt, and pepper and stir to mix. Bring to a simmer and cook 5-6 minutes.

4. In a small bowl, whisk together milk and flour until smooth. Stir into the chicken mixture and cook 3-5 minutes until thickened. Pour into prepared pie plate.

5. Add the rack to the cooking pot. Arrange slices of dough on top of the chicken mixture with widest part of dough on the outside edge.

6. Place the pie on the rack and add the tender-crisp lid. Set to bake on 375°F. Bake 20-25 minutes until crust is golden brown and filling is hot and bubbly. Serve.

Nutrition Info:

• Calories 203,Total Fat 6g,Total Carbs 17g,Protein 21g,Sodium 197mg.

Chicken Chickpea Chili

Servings: 4
Cooking Time: 25 Min

Ingredients:
- 1 pound boneless; skinless chicken breast; cubed /450g
- 2 cans chickpeas, drained and rinsed /435g
- 1 jalapeño pepper; diced
- 1 lime; cut into six wedges
- 3 large serrano peppers; diced
- 1 onion; diced
- ½ cup chopped fresh cilantro /65g
- ½ cup shredded Monterey Jack cheese /65g
- 2 ½ cups water; divided /675ml
- 1 tbsp olive oil /15ml
- 2 tbsp chili powder /30g
- 1 tsp ground cumin /5g
- 1 tsp minced fresh garlic /5g
- 1 tsp salt /5g

Directions:
1. Warm oil on Sear/Sauté. Add in onion, serrano peppers, and jalapeno pepper and cook for 5 minutes until tender; add salt, cumin and garlic for seasoning.
2. Stir chicken with vegetable mixture; cook for 3 to 6 minutes until no longer pink; add 2 cups or 500ml water and chickpeas.
3. Seal the pressure lid, choose Pressure, set to High, and set the timer to 5 minutes. Press Start. Release pressure naturally for 5 minutes. Press Start. Stir chili powder with remaining ½ cup or 125ml water; mix in chili.
4. Press Sear/Sauté. Boil the chili as you stir and cook until slightly thickened. Divide chili into plates; garnish with cheese and cilantro. Over the chili, squeeze a lime wedge.

Tuscan Chicken & Pasta

Servings: 8
Cooking Time: 2 ½ Hours

Ingredients:
- 2½ cups chicken broth, low sodium
- 1 tbsp. Italian seasoning
- ½ tsp salt
- ½ cup mushrooms, sliced
- ¼ tsp crushed red pepper flakes
- 1½ lbs. chicken thighs, boneless, skinless & cut in 1-inch pieces
- ½ lb. macaroni
- ½ cup sun-dried tomatoes with herbs, chopped
- 8 oz. cream cheese, cubed
- 1 cup parmesan cheese
- 1 ½ cups fresh baby spinach

Directions:
1. Spray the cooking pot with cooking spray.
2. Add the broth, Italian seasoning, mushrooms, salt, and pepper flakes to the pot and stir to mix.
3. Stir in chicken. Add the lid and set to slow cook on high. Cook 1 ½ - 2 hours or until chicken is cooked through.
4. Add the pasta and tomatoes and stir to mix. Recover and cook another 25-30 minutes or until pasta is tender, stirring occasionally.
5. Add cream cheese and parmesan and stir until cheeses melt. Stir in spinach and recover. Cook another 5-10 minutes until spinach is wilted and tender. Stir well and serve hot.

Nutrition Info:
- Calories 438,Total Fat 20g,Total Carbs 27g,Protein 35g,Sodium 788mg.

Apricot Bbq Duck Legs

Servings: 6
Cooking Time: 8 Hours

Ingredients:
- Nonstick cooking spray
- 2 cups spicy BBQ sauce
- 1 cup apricot preserves
- 1 tsp ginger
- 1 tbsp. garlic powder
- 2 tbsp. Worcestershire sauce
- 4 lbs. duck legs

Directions:
1. Spray the cooking pot with cooking spray.
2. In a medium bowl, whisk together BBQ sauce, preserves, ginger, garlic powder, and Worcestershire until combined. Reserve ½ cup of the sauce.
3. Add the duck to the cooking pot and pour the sauce over. Stir to coat the duck.
4. Add the lid and select slow cook on low. Cook 6-8 hours or until duck is tender.
5. Add the tender-crisp lid and set to broil. Cook another 2-3 minutes to caramelize the duck legs. Turn the legs over and repeat. Serve.

Nutrition Info:
- Calories 651,Total Fat 26g,Total Carbs 44g,Protein

61g,Sodium 1027mg.

Cheesy Chicken & Mushrooms

Servings: 4
Cooking Time: 30 Minutes

Ingredients:
- Nonstick cooking spray
- 1 ½ cups mushrooms, sliced
- ¼ cup ham, chopped
- 4 chicken breasts, boneless & skinless
- ½ tsp garlic powder
- ¼ tsp pepper
- 1 can cream of chicken soup, reduced fat
- ¾ cup skim milk
- ½ tsp thyme
- ½ tsp onion powder
- ¼ cup mozzarella cheese, grated

Directions:
1. Spray the cooking pot with cooking spray.
2. Set to sauté on med-high heat. Add the mushrooms and ham and cook, stirring occasionally, until mushrooms start to brown, about 5-7 minutes. Transfer to a bowl.
3. Season both sides of the chicken with garlic powder and pepper. Place in the pot. Spoon the mushroom mixture over the top.
4. In a medium bowl, whisk together soup, milk, thyme, and onion powder. Pour over mushrooms and top with cheese.
5. Add the tender-crisp lid and set to bake on 350°F. Cook 25-30 minutes until chicken is cooked through. Serve.

Nutrition Info:
- Calories 243,Total Fat 9g,Total Carbs 9g,Protein 32g,Sodium 987mg.

Chicken Bruschetta

Servings: 4
Cooking Time: 9 Minutes

Ingredients:
- 2 tablespoons balsamic vinegar
- 1/3 cup olive oil
- 2 teaspoons garlic cloves, minced
- 1 teaspoon black pepper
- ½ teaspoon salt
- ½ cup sun-dried tomatoes, in olive oil
- 2 pounds chicken breasts, quartered, boneless

- 2 tablespoons fresh basil, chopped

Directions:
1. Take a suitable and whisk in vinegar, oil, garlic, pepper, salt.
2. Fold in tomatoes, basil and add breast; mix well.
3. Transfer to fridge and let it sit for 30 minutes.
4. Add everything to Ninja Foodi and lock lid, cook on "HIGH" pressure for 9 minutes
5. Quick-release pressure.
6. Serve and enjoy.

Nutrition Info:
- Calories: 480; Fat: 26g; Carbohydrates: 4g; Protein: 52g

Bacon Ranch Chicken Bake

Servings:6
Cooking Time: 30 Minutes

Ingredients:
- 1 pound chicken breast, cut in 1-inch cubes
- 2 tablespoons extra-virgin olive oil
- 3 tablespoons ranch seasoning mix, divided
- 4 strips bacon, chopped
- 1 small onion, chopped
- 2 garlic cloves, minced
- 1 cup long-grain white rice
- 2 cups chicken broth
- ½ cup half-and-half
- 2 cups shredded Cheddar cheese, divided
- 2 tablespoons chopped fresh parsley

Directions:
1. Select SEAR/SAUTÉ and set to HI. Select START/STOP to begin. Let preheat for 5 minutes.
2. In a large bowl, toss the chicken with the olive oil and 2 tablespoons of ranch seasoning mix.
3. Add the bacon to the pot and cook, stirring frequently, for about 6 minutes, or until crispy. Using a slotted spoon, transfer the bacon to a paper towel-lined plate to drain.
4. Add the onion and cook for about 5 minutes. Add the garlic and cook for 1 minute more. Add the chicken and stir, cooking until chicken is cooked through, about 3 minutes.
5. Add the rice, chicken broth, and remaining ranch mix. Assemble pressure lid, making sure the pressure release valve is in the SEAL position.
6. Select PRESSURE and set to HI. Set time to 7 minutes. Select START/STOP to begin.
7. When complete, quick release the pressure by turn-

ing the valve to the VENT position. Carefully remove lid when unit has finished releasing pressure.

8. Stir in half-and-half and 1 cup of Cheddar cheese. Top with the remaining 1 cup of cheese. Close crisping lid.

9. Select BROIL and set time to 8 minutes. Select START/STOP to begin. When cooking is complete, serve garnished with fresh parsley.

Nutrition Info:
• Calories: 512,Total Fat: 27g,Sodium: 999mg,Carbohydrates: 28g,Protein: 35g.

Buttered Turkey

Servings: 6
Cooking Time: 25 Min

Ingredients:
• 6 turkey breasts, boneless and skinless
• 1 stick butter, melted
• 2 cups panko breadcrumbs /260g
• ½ tsp cayenne pepper /2.5g
• ½ tsp black pepper /2.5g
• 1 tsp salt /5g

Directions:
1. In a bowl, combine the panko breadcrumbs, half of the black pepper, the cayenne pepper, and half of the salt.

2. In another bowl, combine the melted butter with salt and pepper. Brush the butter mixture over the turkey breast.

3. Coat the turkey with the panko mixture. Arrange on a lined Foodi basket. Close the crisping lid and cook for 15 minutes at 390 °F or 199°C on Air Crisp mode, flipping the meat after 8 minutes.

Chicken With Roasted Red Pepper Sauce

Servings: 4
Cooking Time: 23 Min

Ingredients:
• 4 chicken breasts; skinless and boneless
• ¼ cup roasted red peppers; chopped /32.5g
• ½ cup chicken broth /125ml
• ½ cup heavy cream /125ml
• 1 tbsp basil pesto /15g
• 1 tbsp cornstarch /15g
• ⅓ tsp Italian Seasoning /1.67g
• ⅓ tsp minced garlic /1.67g

• Salt and black pepper to taste

Directions:
1. In the inner pot of the Foodi, add the chicken at the bottom. Pour the chicken broth and add Italian seasoning, garlic, salt, and pepper.

2. Close the pressure lid, secure the pressure valve, and select Pressure mode on High for 15 minutes. Press Start/Stop.

3. Once the timer has ended, do a natural pressure release for 5 minutes and open the lid. Use a spoon to remove the chicken onto a plate. Scoop out any fat or unwanted chunks from the sauce.

4. In a small bowl, add the cream, cornstarch, red peppers, and pesto. Mix them with a spoon. Pour the creamy mixture into the pot and close the crisping lid.

5. Select Broil mode and cook for 4 minutes. Serve the chicken with sauce over on a bed of cooked quinoa.

Beef, Pork & Lamb

Mississippi Pot Roast With Potatoes 68

Speedy Pork Picante 68

Pork Asado 68

Layered Taco Casserole....69

Lamb Tagine 69

Tender Butter Beef 70

Beef Congee 70

Beef, Barley & Mushroom Stew 70

Beef Mole 71

Beef And Broccoli Sauce .71

Beef Jerky 71

Asian-style Meatballs 72

Honey Short Ribs With Rosemary Potatoes 72

Simple Beef & Shallot Curry 73

Cuban Flank Steak.............73

Brisket Chili Verde 73

Apricot Lemon Ham.........74

Lime Glazed Pork Tenderloin........................74

Corned Beef......................74

Crispy Roast Pork.............75

Polynesian Pork Burger 75

Southern-style Lettuce Wraps................................75

Tamale Pie 76

Beef Stew With Beer 76

Herbed Lamb Chops.........76

Holiday Honey Glazed Ham 77

Sour And Sweet Pork 77

Speedy Pork Stir Fry 77

Butter Pork Chops 78

Zucchini & Beef Lasagna.78

Moroccan Beef 79

Beef Pho With Swiss Chard 79

BEEF, PORK & LAMB

Mississippi Pot Roast With Potatoes

Servings: 6
Cooking Time: 1 Hr 40 Min

Ingredients:
- 2 pounds chuck roast /900g
- 5 potatoes, peeled and sliced
- 10 pepperoncini
- 2 bay leaves
- 1 onion, finely chopped
- ½ cup pepperoncini juice /125ml
- 6 cups beef broth /1500ml
- ¼ cup butter /32.5g
- 1 tbsp canola oil /15ml
- ½ tsp dried thyme /2.5g
- ½ tsp dried parsley /2.5g
- 1 tsp onion powder /5g
- 1 tsp garlic powder /5g
- 2 tsp salt /10g
- ½ tsp black pepper /2.5g

Directions:
1. Warm oil on Sear/Sauté. Season chuck roast with pepper and salt, then sear in the hot oil for 2 to 4 minutes for each side until browned. Set aside.
2. Melt butter and cook onion for 3 minutes until fragrant. Sprinkle with dried parsley, onion powder, dried thyme, and garlic powder and stir for 30 seconds.
3. Into the pot, stir bay leaves, beef broth, pepperoncini juice, and pepperoncini. Nestle chuck roast down into the liquid. Seal the pressure lid, choose Pressure, set to High, and set the timer to 60 minutes. Press Start.
4. Release pressure naturally for about 10 minutes. Set the chuck roast to a cutting board and use two forks to shred. Serve immediately.

Speedy Pork Picante

Servings: 4
Cooking Time: 25 Minutes

Ingredients:
- 2 tbsp. taco seasoning
- 1 lb. pork loin, cut in ¾-inch cubes
- 2 tsp olive oil
- 8 oz. chunky salsa
- 1/3 cup peach preserves

Directions:
1. Place taco seasoning in a large Ziploc bag. Add pork, seal, and turn to coat.
2. Add the oil to the cooking pot and set to sauté on med-high heat.
3. Add the pork and cook,, stirring occasionally, until no longer pink.
4. Add salsa and preserves, reduce heat to med-low, cover, and simmer 15-20 minutes, stirring occasionally.
5. Serve over rice or enjoy as is.

Nutrition Info:
- Calories 234,Total Fat 7g,Total Carbs 15g,Protein 27g,Sodium 764mg.

Pork Asado

Servings: 6
Cooking Time: 1 Hour

Ingredients:
- 1 ½ lbs. pork picnic or shoulder, cut in 2-inch cubes
- ¼ cup soy sauce
- ½ cup lemon juice
- 1 ½ cups water
- ¼ cup olive oil
- 1 onion, peeled & sliced into ¼-inch thick rings
- 2 potatoes, peeled & sliced in ½-inch thick strips
- Salt and pepper to taste

Directions:
1. Add the pork, soy sauce, lemon juice, and water to the cooking pot. Set to sauté on med-high heat and bring to a boil.
2. Add lid and set to pressure cook on high. Set timer for 10 minutes. When timer goes off, use quick release to remove the pressure. Transfer pork and cooking liquid to a bowl.
3. Add the oil to the cooking pot and set to sauté on med-high. Add onions and cook about 1 minute. Use a slotted spoon to transfer them to a bowl.
4. Add potatoes to the pot and cook until tender and lightly browned. Transfer to bowl with onions.
5. Return just the pork to the pot and cook until

browned. Drain off fat. Add the reserved cooking liquid and bring to a boil. Season with salt and pepper. Cook about 5 minutes until liquid is reduced.

6. Place pork on a serving platter and place potatoes and onions around it. Pour the sauce over all and serve.

Nutrition Info:
• Calories 327, Total Fat 13g, Total Carbs 25g, Protein 27g, Sodium 882mg.

Layered Taco Casserole

Servings: 8
Cooking Time: 35 Minutes

Ingredients:
• 2 lbs. lean ground beef
• 1 tsp garlic, chopped fine
• 2 tbsp. chili powder
• 1 tsp onion powder
• ½ cup salsa
• ¼ cup water
• 16 oz. re-fried beans, low fat
• ½ cup sour cream, low fat
• 1 cup cheddar cheese, low fat, grated
• ¼ cup green onion, chopped

Directions:
1. Add the beef to the cooking pot and set to sauté on med-high heat. Cook, breaking up with spatula, until no longer pink. Stir in garlic, chili powder, and onion powder and cook 1 minute more.
2. Stir in salsa and water and cook, stirring occasionally, until liquid has reduced.
3. Spread beans on top of the meat. Top with sour cream then sprinkle the cheese evenly over the top.
4. Add the tender-crisp lid and set to bake on 350°F. Bake 25-30 minutes or until hot and bubbly.
5. Let cool slightly then serve garnished with green onions.

Nutrition Info:
• Calories 360, Total Fat 22g, Total Carbs 11g, Protein 28g, Sodium 513mg.

Lamb Tagine

Servings: 8
Cooking Time: 55 Minutes

Ingredients:
• 1 cup couscous
• 2 cups water
• 3 tablespoons extra-virgin olive oil, divided
• 2 yellow onions, diced
• 3 garlic cloves, minced
• 2 pounds lamb stew meat, cut into 1- to 2-inch cubes
• 1 cup dried apricots, sliced
• 2 cups chicken stock
• 2 tablespoons ras el hanout seasoning
• 1 can chickpeas, drained
• Kosher salt
• Freshly ground black pepper
• 1 cup toasted almonds, for garnish

Directions:
1. Place the couscous in the pot and pour in the water. Assemble pressure lid, making sure the pressure release valve is in the SEAL position.
2. Select PRESSURE and set to HI. Set time to 5 minutes. Select START/STOP to begin.
3. When pressure cooking is complete, quick release the pressure by turning the pressure release valve to the VENT position. Carefully remove lid when unit has finished releasing pressure.
4. Stir 1 tablespoon of oil into the couscous, then transfer the couscous to a bowl.
5. Select SEAR/SAUTÉ and set to MD:HI. Select START/STOP to begin. Let preheat for 3 minutes
6. Add the remaining 2 tablespoons of oil, onion, garlic, and lamb. Sauté for 7 to 10 minutes, stirring frequently.
7. Add the apricots, chicken stock, and ras el hanout. Stir to combine. Assemble pressure lid, making sure the pressure release valve is in the SEAL position.
8. Select PRESSURE and set to HI. Set time to 30 minutes. Select START/STOP to begin.
9. When pressure cooking is complete, quick release the pressure by turning the pressure release valve to the VENT position. Carefully remove lid when unit has finished releasing pressure.
10. Stir in the chickpeas.
11. Select SEAR/SAUTÉ and set to MD:LO. Select START/STOP to begin. Let the mixture simmer for 10 minutes. Season with salt and pepper.
12. When cooking is complete, ladle the tagine over the couscous. Garnish with the toasted almonds.

Nutrition Info:
• Calories: 596, Total Fat: 21g, Sodium: 354mg, Carbohydrates: 65g, Protein: 39g.

Tender Butter Beef

Servings: 12
Cooking Time: 8 Hours

Ingredients:
- 3 lbs. beef stew meat
- 1/3 cup butter
- 1 ¼ oz. dry onion soup mix
- ¼ cup beef broth, low sodium
- 1 tbsp. cornstarch

Directions:
1. Place beef and butter the cooking pot. Sprinkle onion soup mix over the meat.
2. Add the lid and set to slow cook on low. Cook 7-8 hours, stirring occasionally, untl beef is tender.
3. In a small bowl, whisk together broth and cornstarch until smooth. Stir into beef mixture completely and let cook 10 minutes or until sauce has thickened. Serve over cooked rice or quinoa.

Nutrition Info:
- Calories 197,Total Fat 10g,Total Carbs 3g,Protein 25g,Sodium 388mg.

Beef Congee

Servings: 6
Cooking Time: 1 Hr

Ingredients:
- 2 pounds ground beef /900g
- 1 piece fresh ginger; minced
- 2 cloves garlic; minced
- 6 cups beef stock /1500ml
- 1 cup jasmine rice /130g
- 1 cup kale, roughly chopped /130g
- 1 cups water /250ml
- salt and ground black pepper to taste
- Fresh cilantro; chopped

Directions:
1. Run cold water and rinse rice. Add garlic, rice, and ginger into the Foodi. Pour water and stock into the pot and spread the beef on top of rice.
2. Seal the pressure lid, choose Pressure, set to High, and set the timer to 30 minutes. Press Start. Once ready, release pressure naturally for 10 minutes.
3. Stir in kale to obtain the desired consistency. Add pepper and salt for seasoning. Divide into serving plates and top with cilantro.

Beef, Barley & Mushroom Stew

Servings: 8
Cooking Time: 1 Hour 15 Minutes

Ingredients:
- 2 tbsp. butter, unsalted
- 2 lbs. beef chuck, cubed
- 1 tsp salt
- 3 cups onions, chopped
- 1 lb. mushrooms, sliced
- 1 quart beef broth, low sodium
- 3 cups water
- 2 tsp marjoram
- 1 cup pearl barley
- 1 cup carrot, chopped
- 3 cups turnips, peeled & chopped
- ½ tsp pepper
- ½ cup sour cream
- 8 small sprigs fresh dill

Directions:
1. Add the butter to the cooking pot and set to sauté on medium heat.
2. Working in batches, cook the beef until brown on all sides, seasoning with salt as it cooks. Transfer browned beef to a bowl.
3. Add the onions and cook, stirring up brown bits from the bottom of the pot, about 5-6 minutes or until they begin to brown.
4. Add the mushrooms and increase heat to med-high. Cook 2-3 minutes.
5. Add the beef back to the pot and stir in marjoram, broth, and water, stir to mix.
6. Add the lid and set to pressure cook on high. Set timer for 30 minutes. When timer goes off use quick release to remove the pressure.
7. Stir in barley, turnips, and carrots. Add the lid and pressure cook on high another 30 minutes. When the timer goes off, use quick release to remove the pressure.
8. Ladle into bowls and garnish sour cream and dill. Serve immediately.

Nutrition Info:
- Calories 67,Total Fat 2g,Total Carbs 5g,Protein 7g,Sodium 162mg.

Beef Mole

Servings: 8
Cooking Time: 8 Hours

Ingredients:
- 2 lbs. beef stew meat, cut in 1-inch cubes
- 3 tsp salt, divided
- 2 tbsp. olive oil
- 2 onions, chopped fine
- 4 cloves garlic, chopped fine
- 1 chili, seeded & chopped fine
- 3 tsp chili powder
- 1 tsp ancho chili powder
- 2 tsp oregano
- 2 tsp cumin
- 1 tsp paprika
- 1 lb. dried red beans, soaked in water overnight, drained
- 5 cups water
- 2 cups beer
- 2 15 oz. tomatoes, crushed
- 1 tbsp. brown sugar
- 2 oz. unsweetened chocolate, chopped
- 1 bay leaf
- 3 tbsp. lime juice

Directions:
1. Place the beef in a large Ziploc bag with 1 ½ teaspoons salt, seal and rub gently to massage the salt into the meat. Refrigerate overnight.
2. Add the oil to the cooking pot and set to sauté on med-high heat.
3. Working in batches, add the beef and cook until deep brown on all sides. Transfer to a bowl.
4. Add the onions to the pot and cook about 5 minutes or until softened. Stir in garlic, chilies, remaining salt, chili powders, oregano, cumin, and paprika and cook 1 minute more.
5. Stir in beans, water, beer, tomatoes, brown sugar, and chocolate and mix well. Stir in the beef and add the bay leaf.
6. Add the lid and set to slow cook on low. Cook 8 hours or until beef is tender. Stir in lime juice and serve.

Nutrition Info:
- Calories 127,Total Fat 8g,Total Carbs 7g,Protein 7g,Sodium 310mg.

Beef And Broccoli Sauce

Servings: 4
Cooking Time: 35 Min

Ingredients:
- 2 lb. chuck roast, boneless and cut into thin strips /900g
- 4 cloves garlic; minced
- 1 cup beef broth /250ml
- ¾ cup soy sauce /188ml
- 7 cups broccoli florets /910g
- 1 tbsp cornstarch /15g
- 1 tbsp olive oil /15ml
- Salt to taste

Directions:
1. Open the lid of Foodi, and select Sear/Sauté mode. Add the olive oil, and once heated, add the beef and minced garlic. Cook the meat until brown. Stir in soy sauce and beef broth.
2. Close the lid, secure the pressure valve, and select Pressure mode on High pressure for 10 minutes. Press Start/Stop to start cooking.
3. Once the timer has ended, do a quick pressure release and remove the meat and set aside.
4. Use a soup spoon to fetch out a quarter of the liquid into a bowl, add the cornstarch, and mix it until it is well dissolved.
5. Pour the starch mixture into the pot and place the reversible rack. Place the broccoli florets on it and seal the pressure lid. Select Steam mode on LOW for 5 minutes.
6. When ready, do a quick pressure release and open the lid. Remove the rack, stir the sauce, add the meat and close the crisping lid.
7. Cook for 5 minutes on Broil mode. The sauce should be thick enough when you finish cooking. Dish the beef broccoli sauce into a serving bowl and serve with a side of cooked pasta.

Beef Jerky

Servings: 4
Cooking Time: 20 Minutes

Ingredients:
- 1/2-pound beef, sliced into 1/8-inch-thick strips
- 1/2 cup of soy sauce
- 2 tablespoons Worcestershire sauce
- 2 teaspoons black pepper
- 1 teaspoon onion powder

- 1/2 teaspoon garlic powder
- 1 teaspoon salt

Directions:
1. Add listed ingredient to a large-sized Ziploc bag, seal it shut.
2. Shake well, seal and leave it in the fridge overnight.
3. Lay strips on dehydrator trays, making sure not to overlap them.
4. Lock Air Crisping Lid and Set its cooking temperature to 135 °F, cook for 7 hours.

Nutrition Info:
- Calories: 62; Fat: 7g; Carbohydrates: 2g; Protein: 9g

Asian-style Meatballs

Servings:8
Cooking Time: 20 Minutes

Ingredients:
- 1 pound frozen beef meatballs
- 1¼ cups garlic-hoisin sauce
- ¼ cup soy sauce
- ½ cup rice vinegar
- 2 tablespoons brown sugar
- ½ tablespoon sriracha
- 2 tablespoons freshly squeezed lime juice
- 2 tablespoons cornstarch
- 2 tablespoons water
- 1 head butter lettuce

Directions:
1. Place the meatballs, hoisin sauce, soy sauce, rice vinegar, brown sugar, sriracha, and lime juice in the pot and stir. Assemble pressure lid, making sure the pressure release valve is in the SEAL position.
2. Select PRESSURE and set to HI. Set the time to 20 minutes. Select START/STOP to begin.
3. When pressure cooking is complete, quick release the pressure by turning the pressure release valve to the VENT position. Carefully remove the lid when the unit has finished releasing pressure.
4. Transfer the meatballs to a serving bowl.
5. In a small bowl, mix together the cornstarch and water until smooth. Pour this mixture into the pot, whisking it into the sauce. Once sauce has thickened, pour it over the meatballs.
6. Serve the meatballs in lettuce cups with the toppings of your choice, such as sesame seeds, sliced scallions, chopped peanuts, and julienned cucumber.

Nutrition Info:
- Calories: 337,Total Fat: 18g,Sodium: 2070mg,Car-

bohydrates: 41g,Protein: 9g.

Honey Short Ribs With Rosemary Potatoes

Servings: 4
Cooking Time: 105 Min

Ingredients:
- 4 bone-in beef short ribs, silver skin
- 2 potatoes, peeled and cut into 1-inch pieces
- ½ cup beef broth /125ml
- 3 garlic cloves; minced
- 1 onion; chopped
- 2 tbsp olive oil /30ml
- 2 tbsp honey /30ml
- 2 tbsp minced fresh rosemary /30ml
- 1 tsp salt /5g
- 1 tsp black pepper /5g

Directions:
1. Choose Sear/Sauté on the pot and set to High. Choose Start/Stop to preheat the pot. Season the short ribs on all sides with ½ tsp or 2.5g of salt and ½ tsp or 2.5g of pepper. Heat 1 tbsp of olive oil and brown the ribs on all sides, about 10 minutes total. Stir in the onion, honey, broth, 1 tbsp of rosemary, and garlic.
2. Seal the pressure lid, choose Pressure, set to High, and set the time to 40 minutes. Choose Start/Stop to begin. In a large bowl, toss the potatoes with the remaining oil, rosemary, salt, and black pepper.
3. When the ribs are ready, perform a quick pressure release and carefully open the lid.
4. Fix the reversible rack in the higher position of the pot, which is over the ribs. Put the potatoes on the rack. Close the crisping lid. Choose Bake/Roast, set the temperature to 350°F or 177°C, and set the time to 15 minutes. Choose Start/Stop to begin roasting.
5. Once the potatoes are tender and roasted, use tongs to pick the potatoes and the short ribs into a plate; set aside. Choose Sear/Sauté and set to High. Simmer the sauce for 5 minutes and spoon the sauce into a bowl.
6. Allow sitting for 2 minutes and scoop off the fat that forms on top. Serve the ribs with the potatoes and sauce.

Simple Beef & Shallot Curry

Servings: 4
Cooking Time: 40 Minutes

Ingredients:
- 1 lb. beef stew meat
- ¼ tsp salt
- 1/8 tsp turmeric
- 2 tbsp. olive oil
- 2 tbsp. shallots, sliced
- 1 tbsp. fresh ginger, grated
- 1 tbsp. garlic, chopped fine
- 3 cups water
- 2 tsp fish sauce
- 8 shallots, peeled & left whole
- ½ tsp chili powder

Directions:
1. In a large bowl, combine beef, salt, and turmeric, use your fingers to massage the seasonings into the meat. Cover and refrigerate 1 hour.
2. Add the oil to the cooking pot and set to sauté on med-high.
3. Add the sliced shallot and cook until golden brown, 6-8 minutes. Transfer to a bowl.
4. Add the garlic and ginger to the pot and cook 1 minute or until fragrant.
5. Add the beef and cook until no pink shows, about 5-6 minutes. Stir in the water and fish sauce until combined.
6. Add the lid and set to pressure cook on high. Set the timer for 20 minutes. When the timer goes off, use manual release to remove the pressure.
7. Set back to sauté on med-high and add the fried shallots, whole shallots, and chili powder. Cook, stirring frequently, until shallots are soft and sauce has thickened, about 10 minutes. Serve.

Nutrition Info:
- Calories 70, Total Fat 9g, Total Carbs 4g, Protein 7g, Sodium 130mg.

Cuban Flank Steak

Servings: 6
Cooking Time: 8 Hours

Ingredients:
- 15 oz. tomatoes, crushed
- 1 tbsp. apple cider vinegar
- 2 cloves garlic, chopped fine
- 1 tbsp. cumin
- 1 jalapeño, chopped fine
- 2 lbs. flank steak
- 2 red bell peppers, chopped
- 1 onion, chopped
- ½ tsp salt
- ¼ cup black olives, pitted & chopped
- 3 tbsp. green onions, sliced

Directions:
1. Add all ingredients, except the olives, to the cooking pot. Stir to coat.
2. Add the lid and set to slow cook on low. Cook 8 hours or until beef is tender.
3. Transfer beef to a large bowl and shred, using 2 forks. Return the beef to the pot.
4. Add the olives and stir to combine. Serve as is garnished with green onions, or over hot, cooked rice.

Nutrition Info:
- Calories 348, Total Fat 13g, Total Carbs 11g, Protein 45g, Sodium 380mg.

Brisket Chili Verde

Servings: 4
Cooking Time: 19 Minutes

Ingredients:
- 1 tablespoon vegetable oil
- ½ white onion, diced
- 1 jalapeño pepper, diced
- 1 teaspoon garlic, minced
- 1 pound brisket, cooked
- 1 can green chile enchilada sauce
- 1 can fire-roasted diced green chiles
- Juice of 1 lime
- 1 teaspoon seasoning salt
- ½ teaspoon ground chipotle pepper

Directions:
1. Select SEAR/SAUTÉ and set temperature to HI. Select START/STOP to begin and allow to preheat for 5 minutes.
2. Add oil to the pot and allow to heat for 1 minute. Add the onion, jalapeño, and garlic. Sauté for 3 minutes or until onion is translucent.
3. Add the brisket, enchilada sauce, green chiles, lime juice, salt, and chipotle powder. Mix well.
4. Assemble the pressure lid, making sure the pressure release valve is in the SEAL position.
5. Select PRESSURE and set to HI. Set the time to 15 minutes. Select START/STOP to begin.
6. When cooking is complete, quick release the pres-

sure by turning the pressure release valve to the VENT position. Carefully remove the lid when the unit has finished releasing pressure.

Nutrition Info:
- Calories: 427,Total Fat: 16g,Sodium: 1323mg,Carbohydrates: 30g,Protein:41g.

Apricot Lemon Ham

Servings: 12
Cooking Time: 1 Hr

Ingredients:
- 5 pounds smoked ham /2250g
- ¾ cup apricot jam /98g
- ¼ cup water /62.5ml
- ½ cup brown sugar /65g
- Juice from 1 Lime
- ½ tsp ground cardamom /2.5g
- ¼ tsp ground nutmeg /1.25g
- 2 tsp mustard /10g
- freshly ground black pepper to taste

Directions:
1. Into the pot, add water and ham to the steel pot of a pressure cooker. In a bowl, combine jam, lemon juice, cardamom, pepper, nutmeg, mustard, and brown sugar; pour the mixture over the ham. Seal the pressure lid, choose Pressure, set to High, and set the timer to 10 minutes. Press Start.
2. When ready, release the pressure quickly. Transfer the ham to a cutting board; allow to sit for 10 minutes. Press Sear/Sauté.
3. Simmer the liquid and cook for 4 to 6 minutes until thickened into a sauce. Slice ham and place onto a serving bowl. Drizzle with sauce before serving.

Lime Glazed Pork Tenderloin

Servings: 8
Cooking Time: 45 Minutes

Ingredients:
- ¼ cup honey
- 1/3 cup lime juice
- 1 tsp lime zest, grated
- 2 cloves garlic, chopped fine
- 2 tbsp. yellow mustard
- ½ tsp salt
- ½ tsp pepper
- 2 pork tenderloins, 1 lb. each, fat trimmed
- Nonstick cooking spray

Directions:
1. In a large Ziploc bag combine, honey, lime juice, zest, garlic, mustard, salt, and pepper. Seal the bag and shake to mix.
2. Add the tenderloins and turn to coat. Refrigerate overnight.
3. Spray the rack with cooking spray and add it to the cooking pot.
4. Place the tenderloins on the rack, discard marinade. Add the tender-crisp lid and set to roast on 400°F. Cook tenderloins 40-45 minutes or until they reach desired doneness. Transfer to serving plate and let rest 10 minutes before slicing and serving.

Nutrition Info:
- Calories 162,Total Fat 3g,Total Carbs 10g,Protein 24g,Sodium 249mg.

Corned Beef

Servings: 4
Cooking Time: 60 Minutes

Ingredients:
- 4 pounds beef brisket
- 2 garlic cloves, peeled and minced
- 2 yellow onions, peeled and sliced
- 11 ounces celery, sliced
- 1 tablespoon dried dill
- 3 bay leaves
- 4 cinnamon sticks, cut into halves
- Black pepper and salt to taste
- 17 ounces of water

Directions:
1. Take a suitable and stir in beef, add water and cover, let it soak for 2-3 hours.
2. Drain and transfer to the Ninja Foodi.
3. Stir in celery, onions, garlic, bay leaves, dill, cinnamon, dill, salt, pepper and the rest of the water to the Ninja Foodi.
4. Stir and combine it well.
5. Lock and secure the Ninja Foodi's lid, then cook on "HIGH" pressure for 50 minutes.
6. Release pressure naturally over 10 minutes.
7. Transfer meat to cutting board and slice, divide amongst plates and pour the cooking liquid alongside veggies over the servings.
8. Enjoy.

Nutrition Info:
- Calories: 289; Fat: 21g; Carbohydrates: 14g; Protein: 9g

Crispy Roast Pork

Servings: 4
Cooking Time: 50 Min

Ingredients:
- 4 pork tenderloins
- ¾ tsp garlic powder /3.75g
- 1 tsp five spice seasoning /5g
- ½ tsp white pepper /2.5g
- 1 tsp salt /5g
- Cooking spray

Directions:
1. Place the pork, white pepper, garlic powder, five seasoning, and salt into a bowl and toss to coat. Leave to marinate at room temperature for 30 minutes.
2. Place the pork into the Foodi basket, greased with cooking spray, close the crisping lid and cook for 20 minutes at 360 °F or 183°C. After 10 minutes, turn the tenderloins. Serve hot.

Polynesian Pork Burger

Servings: 4
Cooking Time: 25 Minutes

Ingredients:
- 1 lb. ground pork
- ¼ cup green onion, chopped fine
- 1/8 tsp allspice
- 1/8 tsp salt
- 1/8 tsp pepper
- ½ tsp ginger
- 4 pineapple rings
- ¼ cup barbecue sauce
- 4 burger buns
- 4 large lettuce leaves
- ¼ lb. ham, sliced thin

Directions:
1. Spray the rack with cooking spray and place it in the cooking pot.
2. In a large bowl, combine pork, green onion, allspice, salt, pepper, and ginger until thoroughly mixed. Form into 4 patties.
3. Place the patties on the rack and brush the tops with barbecue sauce. Add the tender-crisp lid and set to broil. Cook patties 5-7 minutes, flip and brush with barbecue sauce, cook another 5-7 minutes. Place the patties on the bottom of the cooking pot.
4. Spray the rack with cooking spray again. Lay the pineapple rings on the rack. Cook 3-5 minutes per side. Transfer pineapple and patties to a serving plate and let sit 5 minutes.
5. Place the buns on the rack, cut side up, and toast. To serve; top bottom bun with lettuce, then patty, barbecue sauce, ham, pineapple and top bun. Repeat. Serve immediately.

Nutrition Info:
- Calories 155,Total Fat 7g,Total Carbs 13g,Protein 10g,Sodium 279mg.

Southern-style Lettuce Wraps

Servings:6
Cooking Time: 30 Minutes

Ingredients:
- 3 pounds boneless pork shoulder, cut into 1- to 2-inch cubes
- 2 cups light beer
- 1 cup brown sugar
- 1 teaspoon chipotle chiles in adobo sauce
- 1 cup barbecue sauce
- 1 head iceberg lettuce, quartered and leaves separated
- 1 cup roasted peanuts, chopped or ground
- Cilantro leaves

Directions:
1. Place the pork, beer, brown sugar, chipotle, and barbecue sauce in the pot. Assemble pressure lid, making sure the pressure release valve is in the SEAL position.
2. Select PRESSURE and set to HI. Set the timer to 30 minutes. Select START/STOP to begin.
3. When pressure cooking is complete, quick release the pressure by turning the pressure release valve to the VENT position. Carefully remove lid when unit has finished releasing pressure.
4. Using a silicone-tipped utensil, shred the pork in the pot. Stir to mix the meat in with the sauce.
5. Place a small amount of pork in a piece of lettuce. Top with peanuts and cilantro to serve.

Nutrition Info:
- Calories: 811,Total Fat: 58g,Sodium: 627mg,Carbohydrates: 22g,Protein: 45g.

Tamale Pie

Servings: 8
Cooking Time: 8 Hours

Ingredients:
- 1 lb. lean ground beef
- 16 oz. salsa
- 1 carrot, peeled & chopped fine
- 15 oz. black beans, drained & rinsed
- 4 ½ oz. green chilies, diced, divided
- 1 ½ cups fresh corn
- 1 tsp cumin
- 2 tsp chili powder
- 1 tsp salt, divided
- ¾ tsp pepper, divided
- 1 ¼ cups cheddar cheese, low fat, grated, divided
- 1 cup cornmeal
- 1 tsp baking powder
- ½ tsp baking soda
- 1 egg
- ¾ cup low-fat buttermilk

Directions:
1. Add the ground beef to the cooking pot and set to sauté on med-high heat. Cook, breaking up with a spatula until meat is no longer pink. Drain the fat.
2. Stir in salsa, carrots, beans, half the green chilies, corn, cumin, chili powder, ½ teaspoon salt, ½ teaspoon pepper, ½ cup of the cheese, mix well.
3. In a medium bowl, combine corn meal, baking powder, baking soda, remaining salt and pepper, mix well.
4. Add the egg, buttermilk, remaining chilies, and ½ cup cheese, stir just until combined. Spread evenly over the meat mixture. Sprinkle remaining cheese over the top.
5. Add the lid and set to slow cook on low and cook 6-8 hours until filling is hot and bubbly and top crust is cooked through. Serve.

Nutrition Info:
- Calories 407,Total Fat 20g,Total Carbs 38g,Protein 21g,Sodium 324mg.

Beef Stew With Beer

Servings: 4
Cooking Time: 60 Min

Ingredients:
- 2 lb. beef stewed meat; cut into bite-size pieces /900g
- 1 packet dry onion soup mix
- 2 cloves garlic; minced
- 2 cups beef broth /500ml
- ¼ cup flour /32.5g
- 1 medium bottle beer
- 3 tbsp butter/45g
- 2 tbsp Worcestershire sauce /30ml
- 1 tbsp tomato paste /15g
- Salt and black pepper to taste

Directions:
1. In a zipper bag, add beef, salt, all-purpose flour, and pepper. Close the bag up and shake it to coat the meat well with the mixture. Select Sear/Sauté mode on the Foodi. Melt the butter, and brown the beef on both sides, for 5 minutes.
2. Pour the broth to deglaze the bottom of the pot. Stir in tomato paste, beer, Worcestershire sauce, and the onion soup mix.
3. Close the lid, secure the pressure valve, and select Pressure mode on High pressure for 25 minutes. Press Start/Stop to start cooking.
4. Once the timer is done, do a natural pressure release for 10 minutes, and then a quick pressure release to let out any remaining steam.
5. Open the pressure lid and close the crisping lid. Cook on Broil mode for 10 minutes. Spoon the beef stew into serving bowls and serve with over a bed of vegetable mash with steamed greens.

Herbed Lamb Chops

Servings: 4
Cooking Time: 30 Min

Ingredients:
- 4 lamb chops
- 1 garlic clove, peeled
- ½ tbsp oregano /2.5g
- 1 tbsp plus /5g
- ½ tbsp thyme /2.5g
- 2 tsp olive oil /10ml
- ½ tsp salt /2.5g
- ¼ tsp black pepper /1.25g

Directions:

1. Coat the garlic clove with 1 tsp of olive oil and cook in the Foodi for 10 minutes on Air Crisp mode. Meanwhile, mix the herbs and seasonings with the remaining olive oil.

2. Using a towel, squeeze the hot roasted garlic clove into the herb mixture and stir to combine. Coat the lamb chops with the mixture well, and place in the Foodi.

3. Close the crisping lid and cook for about 8 to 12 minutes on Air Crisp mode at 390 °F or 199°C, until crispy on the outside.

Holiday Honey Glazed Ham

Servings: 10
Cooking Time: 30 Min

Ingredients:

- 1 ham, bone-in /2250g
- ¼ cup brown sugar /32.5g
- ½ cup apple cider /125ml
- ¼ cup honey /62.5ml
- 1 pinch ground cloves
- 2 tbsp orange juice /30ml
- 1 tbsp Dijon mustard /15ml
- 2 tbsp pineapple juice (optional) /30ml
- ¼ tsp grated nutmeg /32.5g
- ½ tsp ground cinnamon /2.5g

Directions:

1. Set on Sear/Sauté, set to Medium High, and choose Start/Stop to preheat the pot. Press Start. Mix in apple cider, mustard, pineapple juice, cloves, cinnamon, brown sugar, honey, orange juice, and nutmeg; cook until sauce becomes warm and the sugar and spices are completely dissolved.

2. Lay ham into the sauce. Seal the pressure lid, choose Pressure, set to High, and set the timer to 10 minutes; press Start. When ready, release the pressure quickly.

3. As the ham cooks, preheat the oven's broiler. Line aluminum foil to a baking sheet. Transfer the ham to the prepared baking sheet. On Sear/Sauté, cook the remaining liquid for 4 to 6 minutes until you have a thick and syrupy glaze. Brush the glaze onto ham.

4. Set the glazed ham in the preheated broiler and bake for 3 to 5 minutes until the glaze is caramelized. Place the ham on a cutting board and slice. Transfer to a serving bowl and drizzle glaze over the ham.

Sour And Sweet Pork

Servings: 4
Cooking Time: 40 Min

Ingredients:

- 1 pound pork loin; cut into chunks /450g
- 15 ounces canned peaches /450g
- ¼ cup water /62.5ml
- ¼ cup beef stock /62.5ml
- 2 tbsp sweet chili sauce /30ml
- 2 tbsp soy sauce /30ml
- 2 tbsp cornstarch /30g
- 2 tbsp white wine /30ml
- 2 tbsp honey /30ml

Directions:

1. Into the pot, mix soy sauce, beef stock, white wine, juice from the canned peaches, and sweet chili sauce; stir in pork to coat.

2. Seal the pressure lid, choose Pressure, set to High, and set the timer to 5 minutes. Press Start. Release pressure naturally for 10 minutes, then release the remaining pressure quickly. Remove the pork to a serving plate. Chop the peaches into small pieces.

3. In a bowl, mix water and cornstarch until cornstarch dissolves completely; stir the mixture into the pot. Press Sear/Sauté and cook for 5 more minutes until you obtain the desired thick consistency; add in the chopped peaches and stir well. Serve the pork topped with peach sauce and enjoy.

Speedy Pork Stir Fry

Servings: 4
Cooking Time: 5 Minutes

Ingredients:

- 2 tbsp. soy sauce, low sodium
- 1 tsp sugar
- 1 tsp cornstarch
- 1 lb. pork loin, cut in ¼-inch strips
- 4 tbsp. peanut oil
- 5 cloves garlic, sliced thin
- 1 tsp. red pepper flakes
- 10 green onions, sliced
- ½ tsp sesame oil

Directions:

1. In a large bowl, whisk together soy sauce, sugar, and cornstarch until smooth.

2. Add the pork to the bowl and toss to coat. Let sit for 10 minutes.

3. Add the oil to the cooking pot and set to sauté on med-high heat.

4. Add the garlic and pepper flakes and cook, stirring, about 30 seconds or until garlic starts to brown.

5. Add the pork mixture and cook until meat is no longer pink, stirring constantly.

6. Add the green onions and cook 1 minute more. Turn off the heat and stir in the sesame oil. Serve as is or over hot, cooked rice.

Nutrition Info:
• Calories 182, Total Fat 12g, Total Carbs 3g, Protein 15g, Sodium 279mg.

Butter Pork Chops

Servings: 4
Cooking Time: 10 Minutes

Ingredients:
• 4 pork chops
• Black pepper and salt, to taste
• 2 tablespoons butter
• 2 teaspoons garlic, minced
• 1/2 cup herbed chicken stock
• 1/2 cup heavy whip cream
• 1/2 a lemon, juiced

Directions:
1. Season the four pork chops with black pepper and salt.

2. Select "Sauté" mode on Ninja Foodi and add oil to heat up.

3. Add pork chops and sauté both sides until the golden, total for 6 minutes.

4. Remove thighs to a platter and keep it on the side.

5. Add garlic and cook for 2 minutes.

6. Whisk in chicken stock, heavy cream, lemon juice and bring the sauce to simmer and reintroduce the pork chops.

7. Lock and secure the Ninja Foodi's lid and cook for 10 minutes on "HIGH" pressure.

8. Release pressure naturally over 10 minutes.

9. Serve warm and enjoy.

Nutrition Info:
• Calories: 294; Fat: 26g; Carbohydrates: 4g; Protein: 12g

Zucchini & Beef Lasagna

Servings: 4
Cooking Time: 1 Hour

Ingredients:
• 2 zucchini, cut lengthwise in ½-thick slices
• ½ tsp salt
• Nonstick cooking spray
• 3 tomatoes
• 1 cup onion, chopped
• 2 cloves garlic, chopped fine
• 1 serrano chili, chopped fine
• 1 ½ cups mushrooms, chopped
• 1 lb. lean ground beef
• ½ cube chicken bouillon
• 1 tsp paprika
• 1 tsp thyme
• 1 tsp basil
• ½ tsp salt
• ¼ tsp pepper
• ½ cup mozzarella cheese, grated

Directions:
1. Place zucchini in a large bowl, sprinkle with salt and let sit 10 minutes.

2. Spray the rack with cooking spray and add it to the cooking pot. Pat zucchini dry with paper towels and lay them on the rack, these will need to be done in batches. Add the tender-crisp lid and set to broil, cook zucchini 3 minutes. Transfer to a paper-towel lined baking sheet.

3. Bring a pot of water to a boil. Cut the ends off the tomatoes and make an X insertion on the top. Place in boiling water for 2-3 minutes. Transfer to bowl of ice water and remove the skin. Chop the tomatoes.

4. Spray the cooking pot with cooking spray and set to sauté on med-high heat. Add onion, garlic, and chili and cook 1 minute. Add the tomatoes and mushrooms and cook 3-4 minutes or until almost tender. Transfer to a bowl.

5. Add the beef to the cooking pot and cook, breaking up with a spatula, until no longer pink.

6. Add the vegetables to the beef along with the bouillon and remaining spices. Reduce heat to low and simmer 25 minutes, stirring occasionally.

7. Spray an 8x8-inch baking dish with cooking spray. Lay 1/3 of the zucchini across the bottom. Top with 1/3 of the meat mixture. Repeat layers two more times. Sprinkle cheese evenly over the top.

8. Add the rack back to the cooking pot and place la-

sagna on it. Add the tender-crisp lid and set to bake on 375°F. Bake 35 minutes. Transfer to cutting board and let rest 10 minutes before serving.

Nutrition Info:
- Calories 309, Total Fat 18g, Total Carbs 9g, Protein 28g, Sodium 775mg.

Moroccan Beef

Servings: 10
Cooking Time: 7 Hours 40 Minutes

Ingredients:
- 2 lbs. beef chuck roast, cubed
- 1 tbsp. salt
- 1 tbsp. butter, unsalted
- 2 tomatoes, sliced
- 2 tbsp. honey
- 1 tbsp. harissa paste
- 1 tbsp. tablespoon ras el hanout
- ½ tsp cinnamon
- ½ lb. dried apricots, sliced
- 1 yellow bell pepper, seeded & sliced
- 1 cup onion, sliced thin
- 3 cloves garlic, chopped
- ¼ cup dates, chopped
- 2 cups rice, cooked
- ¼ cup cilantro, chopped
- ¼ cup sesame seeds, toasted

Directions:
1. Season meat with salt and mix well.
2. Add the butter to the cooking pot and set to sauté on med-high heat.
3. Once butter has melted, add meat and cook, stirring occasionally, until browned on all sides.
4. In a large bowl, combine tomatoes, honey, harissa, ras el hanout seasoning, and cinnamon, mix well. Stir in apricots, bell pepper, onion, garlic, and dates. Pour over the beef.
5. Add the lid and set to slow cook on low. Cook 7-9 hours until beef and vegetables are tender.
6. Divide rice evenly among serving plates. Top with beef mixture and garnish with cilantro and sesame seeds. Serve.

Nutrition Info:
- Calories 456, Total Fat 12g, Total Carbs 61g, Protein 29g, Sodium 992mg.

Beef Pho With Swiss Chard

Servings: 6
Cooking Time: 1 Hr 10 Min

Ingredients:
- 2 pounds Beef Neck Bones /900g
- 10 ounces sirloin steak /300g
- 8 ounces rice noodles /240g
- 1 yellow onion, quartered
- A handful of fresh cilantro; chopped
- 2 scallions; chopped
- 2 jalapeño peppers; sliced
- ¼ cup minced fresh ginger /32.5g
- 9 cups water /2250ml
- 2 cups Swiss chard; chopped /260g
- 2 tsp coriander seeds /10g
- 2 tsp ground cinnamon /10g
- 2 tsp ground cloves /10g
- 2 tbsp coconut oil /30ml
- 3 tbsp sugar /45g
- 2 tbsp fish sauce /30ml
- 2 ½ tsp kosher salt /12.5g
- Freshly ground black pepper to taste

Directions:
1. Melt the oil on Sear/Sauté. Add ginger and onions and cook for 4 minutes until the onions are softened. Stir in cloves, cinnamon and coriander seeds and cook for 1 minute until soft. Add in water, salt, beef meat and bones.
2. Seal the pressure lid, choose Pressure, set to High, and set the timer to 30 minutes. Press Start. Release pressure naturally for 10 minutes.
3. Transfer the meat to a large bowl; cover with it enough water and soak for 10 minutes. Drain the water and slice the beef. In hot water, soak rice noodles for 8 minutes until softened and pliable; drain and rinse with cold water. Drain liquid from cooker into a separate pot through a fine-mesh strainer; get rid of any solids.
4. Add fish sauce and sugar to the broth; transfer into the Foodi and simmer on Sear/Sauté. Place the noodles in four separate soup bowls. Top with steak slices, scallions, swiss chard; sliced jalapeño pepper, cilantro, red onion, and pepper. Spoon the broth over each bowl to serve.

Fish & Seafood

Air Fried Scallops............81
Farfalle Tuna Casserole With Cheese 81
Kung Pao Shrimp 81
Seafood Gumbo................82
Citrus Glazed Halibut.......82
Seared Scallops In Asparagus Sauce 83
Spanish Steamed Clams ...83
Mediterranean Cod...........83
Easy Clam Chowder.........84
Steamed Sea Bass With Turnips.............................84
Tilapia With Spicy Pesto ..84
Shrimp And Sausage Paella85
Stir Fried Scallops & Veggies 85
Blackened Salmon............85
Coconut Shrimp With Pineapple Rice..................86
Pistachio Crusted Mahi Mahi 86

Tuna Patties 87
Flounder Veggie Soup 87
Oyster Stew 87
Tangy Catfish & Mushrooms 87
Succotash With Basil Crusted Fish 88
Sweet & Spicy Shrimp Bowls 88
Fish Broccoli Stew 89
Caramelized Salmon.........89
Panko Crusted Cod...........89
Crab Alfredo 90
Almond Crusted Haddock 90
Crab Cake Casserole 90
Salmon With Creamy Grits91
Italian Flounder 91
Clam Fritters....................92
Drunken Saffron Mussels .92

Air Fried Scallops

Servings: 4
Cooking Time: 5 Minutes

Ingredients:
- 12 scallops
- 3 tablespoons olive oil
- Black pepper and salt, to taste

Directions:
1. Rub the scallops with salt, pepper and olive oil.
2. Transfer it to Ninja foodi.
3. Place the insert in your Ninja foodi.
4. Close the air crisping lid.
5. Cook for 4 minutes to 390°F.
6. Flip them after 2 minutes.
7. Serve and enjoy.

Nutrition Info:
- Calories: 372g; Fat: 11g; Carbohydrates: 0.9g; Protein: 63g

Farfalle Tuna Casserole With Cheese

Servings: 4
Cooking Time: 60 Min

Ingredients:
- 6 ounces farfalle /180g
- 1 can full cream milk; divided /360ml
- 2 cans tuna, drained /180g
- 1 medium onion; chopped
- 1 large carrot; chopped
- 1 cup vegetable broth /250ml
- 2 cups shredded Monterey Jack cheese /260g
- 1 cup chopped green beans /130g
- 2½ cups panko bread crumbs /325g
- 3 tbsps butter, melted /45ml
- 1 tbsp olive oil/ 15ml
- 1 tsp salt/ 5g
- 2 tsp s corn starch /10g

Directions:
1. On the Foodi, Choose Sear/Sauté and adjust to Medium. Press Start to preheat the pot.
2. Heat the oil until shimmering and sauté the onion and carrots for 3 minutes, stirring, until softened.
3. Add the farfalle, ¾ cup or 188ml of milk, broth,

and salt to the pot. Stir to combine and submerge the farfalle in the liquid with a spoon.
4. Seal the pressure lid, choose pressure; adjust the pressure to Low and the cook time to 5 minutes; press Start. After cooking, do a quick pressure release and carefully open the pressure lid.
5. Choose Sear/Sauté and adjust to Less for low heat. Press Start. Pour the remaining milk on the farfalle.
6. In a medium bowl, mix the cheese and cornstarch evenly and add the cheese mixture by large handfuls to the sauce while stirring until the cheese melts and the sauce thickens. Add the tuna and green beans, gently stir. Heat for 2 minutes.
7. In another bowl, mix the crumbs and melted butter well. Spread the crumbs over the casserole. Close the crisping lid and press Broil. Adjust the cook time to 5 minutes; press Start. When ready, the topping should be crisp and brown. If not, broil for 2 more minutes. Serve immediately.

Kung Pao Shrimp

Servings: 4
Cooking Time: 15 Minutes

Ingredients:
- 1 tbsp. olive oil
- 1 red bell pepper, seeded & chopped
- 1 green bell pepper, seeded & chopped
- 3 cloves garlic, chopped fine
- 1 lb. large shrimp, peeled & deveined
- ¼ cup soy sauce
- 1 tsp sesame oil
- 1 tsp brown sugar
- 1 tsp Sriracha
- 1/8 tsp red pepper flakes
- 1 tsp cornstarch
- 1 tbsp. water
- ¼ cup peanuts
- ¼ cup green onions, sliced thin

Directions:
1. Add oil to the cooking pot and set to sauté on med-high heat.
2. Add the bell peppers and garlic and cook, 3-5 minutes, until pepper is almost tender.
3. Add the shrimp and cook until they turn pink, 2-3

minutes.

4. In a small bowl, whisk together soy sauce, sesame oil, brown sugar, Sriracha, and pepper flakes until combined.

5. In a separate small bowl, whisk together cornstarch and water until smooth. Whisk into sauce and pour over shrimp mixture. Add the peanuts.

6. Cook, stirring, until the sauce has thickened, about 2-3 minutes. Serve garnished with green onions.

Nutrition Info:
• Calories 212,Total Fat 11g,Total Carbs 10g,Protein 20g,Sodium 1729mg.

Seafood Gumbo

Servings: 4
Cooking Time: 90 Min

Ingredients:
• 1 pound jumbo shrimp /450g
• 8 ounces lump crabmeat /240g
• 1 medium onion; chopped
• 2 green onions, finely sliced
• 1 small banana pepper, seeded and minced
• 1 small red bell pepper; chopped (about ⅔ cup)
• 2 celery stalks; chopped
• 2 garlic cloves, minced
• 3 cups chicken broth /750ml
• ¼ cup olive oil, plus 2 tsp s /72.5ml
• ⅓ cup all-purpose flour /44g
• 1 cup jasmine rice /130g
• ¾ cup water /375ml
• 1½ tsp s Cajun Seasoning /7.5g
• 1½ tsp s salt divided /7.5g

Directions:
1. Lay the shrimp in the Crisping Basket. Season with ½ tsp or 2.5g of salt and 2 tsp s or 10ml of olive oil. Toss to coat and fix the basket in the inner pot. Close the crisping lid and Choose Air Crisp; adjust the temperature to 400°F or 205°C and the cook time to 6 minutes. Press Start.

2. After 3 minutes, open the lid and toss the shrimp. Close the lid and resume cooking. When ready, the shrimp should be opaque and pink. Remove the basket and set aside.

3. Choose Sear/Sauté and adjust to High. Press Start. Heat the remaining ¼ cup of olive oil. Whisk in the flour with a wooden spoon and cook the roux that forms for 3 to 5 minutes, stirring constantly, until the roux has the color of peanut butter. Turn the pot off.

4. Stir in the Cajun, onion, bell pepper, celery, garlic, and banana pepper for about 5 minutes until the mixture slightly cools. Add the chicken broth and crabmeat, stir.

5. Put the rice into a heatproof bowl. Add the water and the remaining salt. Cover the bowl with foil. Put the reversible rack in the lower position of the pot and set the bowl in the rack.

6. Seal the pressure lid, choose Pressure; adjust the pressure to High and the cook time to 6 minutes; press Start. After cooking, perform a natural pressure for 8 minutes. Take out the rack and bowl and set aside. Stir the shrimp into the gumbo to heat it up for 3 minutes.

7. Fluff the rice with a fork and divide into the center of four bowls. Spoon the gumbo around the rice and garnish with the green onions.

Citrus Glazed Halibut

Servings: 4
Cooking Time: 10 Minutes

Ingredients:
• Nonstick cooking spray
• 1 onion, chopped
• 1 clove garlic, chopped fine
• 4 halibut steaks
• ½ tsp salt
• ¼ tsp lemon-pepper
• ½ cup fresh orange juice
• 1 tbsp. fresh lemon juice
• 2 tbsp. fresh parsley, chopped fine

Directions:
1. Spray the cooking pot with cooking spray. Set to sauté on medium heat.

2. Add the onion and garlic and cook 2-3 minutes until onion starts to soften.

3. Add the halibut and season with salt and pepper. Drizzle the orange and lemon juices over the fish and sprinkle with parsley.

4. Add the lid and reduce heat to med-low. Cook 10-12 minutes until fish flakes easily with a fork. Serve immediately.

Nutrition Info:
• Calories 131,Total Fat 2g,Total Carbs 6g,Protein 22g,Sodium 370mg.

Seared Scallops In Asparagus Sauce

Servings: 2
Cooking Time: 25 Minutes

Ingredients:
- 10 sea scallops
- Salt
- 1 lb. asparagus, trimmed
- ¼ cup chicken broth, low sodium
- 2 tbsp. olive oil
- 2-3 tablespoons butter

Directions:
1. Salt both sides of the scallops and set aside.
2. Fill the cooking pot half full with water. Set to sauté on high heat and bring to a boil.
3. Peel off the outer layer of asparagus spears. Chop into 2-inch pieces. When water is boiling add asparagus and cook 5-8 minutes.
4. Transfer asparagus to a food processor or blender. Add half the broth and process until smooth. Discard the water in the pot.
5. Add oil to the cooking pot and set to med-high heat. Let oil heat for 2 minutes.
6. Pat scallops dry with paper towel and lay in the pot, don't overcrowd them. Let cook 3-4 minutes. When you see a golden brown ring on the bottom edge of the scallop, turn them over. Sear another 1-2 minutes. Transfer to a plate and cover to keep warm.
7. Decrease the heat to med-low and pour the pureed asparagus in the pot. Add the butter and cook, stirring until butter melts, do not let it boil. Add salt to taste.
8. To serve, spoon sauce on the bottom of serving plates and top with scallops. Serve immediately.

Nutrition Info:
- Calories 91, Total Fat 8g, Total Carbs 3g, Protein 3g, Sodium 214mg.

Spanish Steamed Clams

Servings: 6
Cooking Time: 20 Minutes

Ingredients:
- 3 tbsp. olive oil
- 1 onion, chopped fine
- 3 oz. prosciutto, chopped
- ¼ cup dry sherry
- 36 littleneck clams

Directions:
1. Add the oil to the cooking pot and set to sauté on med-high heat.
2. Add the onion and cook, stirring, 1 minutes. Reduce heat to low, add the lid and cook 10-15 minutes until onion is soft.
3. Stir in remaining ingredients and increase heat to medium. Add the lid and cook 5 minutes, or until the clams open.
4. Discard any unopened clams and serve immediately.

Nutrition Info:
- Calories 166, Total Fat 9g, Total Carbs 5g, Protein 15g, Sodium 657mg.

Mediterranean Cod

Servings: 4
Cooking Time: 20 Min

Ingredients:
- 4 fillets cod
- 1 bunch fresh thyme sprigs
- 1 pound cherry tomatoes, halved /450g
- 1 clove garlic, pressed
- 1 cup white rice /130g
- 2 cups water /500ml
- 1 cup Kalamata olives /130g
- 2 tbsp pickled capers /30g
- 1 tbsp olive oil; divided /15ml
- 1 tsp olive oil /15ml
- 1 pinch ground black pepper
- 3 pinches salt

Directions:
1. Line a parchment paper to the steamer basket of your Foodi. Place about half the tomatoes in a single layer on the paper. Sprinkle with thyme, reserving some for garnish. Arrange cod fillets on the top of tomatoes. Sprinkle with a little bit of olive oil.
2. Spread the garlic, pepper, salt, and remaining tomatoes over the fish. In the pot, mix rice and water. Lay a trivet over the rice and water. Lower steamer basket onto the trivet.
3. Seal the pressure lid, choose Pressure, set to High, and set the timer to 7 minutes. Press Start. When ready, release the pressure quickly.
4. Remove the steamer basket and trivet from the pot. Use a fork to fluff rice. Plate the fish fillets and apply a garnish of olives, reserved thyme, pepper, remaining olive oil, and capers. Serve with rice.

Easy Clam Chowder

Servings: 6
Cooking Time: 3 Hours

Ingredients:
- 5 slices bacon, chopped
- 2 cloves garlic, chopped fine
- ½ onion, chopped
- ½ tsp thyme
- 1 cup chicken broth, low sodium
- 4 oz. cream cheese
- 18 oz. clams, chopped & drained
- 1 bay leaf
- 3 cups cauliflower, separated in florets
- 1 cup almond milk, unsweetened
- 1 cup heavy cream
- 2 tbsp. fresh parsley, chopped

Directions:
1. Add the bacon to the cooking pot and set to sauté on med-high heat. Cook until crisp, transfer to a pa-per-towel lined plate. Pour out all but 3 tablespoons of the fat.
2. Add the onion and garlic and cook 2-3 minutes until onion is translucent. Add the thyme and cook 1 minute more.
3. Add the broth, cream cheese, clams, bay leaf, and cauliflower, mix until combined. Add the lid and set to slow cook on low. Cook 2-3 hours until cauliflower is tender. Stir in the milk and cream and cook until heat-ed through.
4. Ladle into bowls and top with bacon and parsley. Serve warm.

Nutrition Info:
- Calories 377,Total Fat 24g,Total Carbs 13g,Protein 27g,Sodium 468mg.

Steamed Sea Bass With Turnips

Servings: 4
Cooking Time: 15 Min

Ingredients:
- 4 sea bass fillets
- 4 sprigs thyme
- 1 lemon; sliced
- 2 turnips; sliced
- 1 white onion; sliced into thin rings
- 1½ cups water /375ml
- 2 tsp olive oil /30ml
- 2 pinches salt

- 1 pinch ground black pepper

Directions:
1. Add water to the Foodi. Set a reversible rack into the pot. Line a parchment paper to the bottom of steamer basket. Place lemon slices in a single layer on the reversible rack.
2. Arrange fillets on the top of the lemons, cover with onion and thyme sprigs and top with turnip slices.
3. Drizzle pepper, salt, and olive oil over the mixture. Put steamer basket onto the reversible rack. Seal lid and cook on Low for 8 minutes; press Start.
4. When ready, release pressure quickly. Serve over the delicate onion rings and thinly sliced turnips.

Tilapia With Spicy Pesto

Servings: 4
Cooking Time: 10 Minutes

Ingredients:
- Nonstick cooking spray
- 1 cup cilantro, packed
- 3 cloves garlic
- 2 tbsp. fresh lemon juice
- ¼ tsp salt
- 1/8 tsp red pepper
- 2 tbsp. olive oil
- 4 tilapia fillets

Directions:
1. Place the rack in the cooking pot. Spray a baking pan with cooking spray.
2. Place everything but the fish and oil in a food pro-cessor or blender and pulse until well chopped.
3. Slowly add the oil, with machine running, until combined.
4. Place the fish in the prepared pan and spread the pesto evenly over the top. Place on the rack.
5. Add the tender-crisp lid and set to bake on 400°F. Bake 10-12 minutes until fish flakes with a fork. Serve immediately.

Nutrition Info:
- Calories 174,Total Fat 9g,Total Carbs 1g,Protein 23g,Sodium 207mg.

Shrimp And Sausage Paella

Servings: 4
Cooking Time: 70 Min

Ingredients:
- 1 pound andouille sausage; sliced /450g
- 1 pound baby squid, cut into ¼-inch rings /450g
- 1 pound jumbo shrimp, peeled and deveined /450g
- 1 white onion; chopped
- 4 garlic cloves, minced
- 1 red bell pepper; diced
- 2 cups Spanish rice /260g
- 4 cups chicken stock /1000ml
- ½ cup dry white wine /125ml
- 1 tbsp melted butter /15ml
- 1 tsp turmeric powder /5g
- 1½ tsp s sweet paprika /7.5g
- ½ tsp freshly ground black pepper /5g
- ½ tsp salt /5g

Directions:
1. Choose Sear/Sauté on the pot and set to Medium High. Choose Start/Stop to preheat the pot. Melt the butter and add the sausage. Cook until browned on both sides, about 3 minutes while stirring frequently. Remove the sausage to a plate and set aside.
2. Sauté the onion and garlic in the same fat for 3 minutes until fragrant and pour in the wine. Use a wooden spoon to scrape the bottom of the pot of any brown bits and cook for 2 minutes or until the wine reduces by half.
3. Stir in the rice and water. Season with the paprika, turmeric, black pepper, and salt. Seal the pressure lid, choose Pressure and set to High. Set the time to 5 minutes, then Choose Start/Stop. When done cooking, do a quick pressure release and carefully open the lid.
4. Choose Sear/Sauté, set to Medium High, and choose Start/Stop. Add the squid and shrimp to the pot and stir gently without mashing the rice.
5. Seal the pressure lid again and cook for 6 minutes, until the shrimp are pink and opaque. Return the sausage to the pot and mix in the bell pepper. Warm through for 2 minutes. Dish the paella and serve immediately.

Stir Fried Scallops & Veggies

Servings: 6
Cooking Time: 15 Minutes

Ingredients:
- 2 tbsp. peanut oil
- 3 cloves garlic, chopped fine
- 1 tsp crushed red pepper flakes
- 1 lb. bay scallops
- 2 tbsp. sesame seeds
- 1 ½ tsp ginger
- 1 head bok choy, trimmed and chopped
- 16 oz. stir-fry vegetables
- 1 tbsp. soy sauce, low sodium

Directions:
1. Add the oil to the cooking pot and set to saute on med-high heat.
2. Add the garlic, red pepper flakes, and scallops and cook until scallops are golden brown and cooked. Transfer scallops to a bowl and keep warm.
3. Add the sesame seeds and ginger and cook, stirring, 1-2 minutes until all the liquid is gone.
4. Add the cabbage and vegetables and cook 4-5 minutes, stirring occasionally.
5. Add the soy sauce and return the scallops to the pot. Cook 1-2 minutes more until heated through. Serve immediately.

Nutrition Info:
- Calories 172,Total Fat 5g,Total Carbs 17g,Protein 15g,Sodium 485mg.

Blackened Salmon

Servings: 4
Cooking Time: 10 Minutes

Ingredients:
- 1 tbsp. plus 1 tsp sweet paprika
- 1 tsp garlic powder
- 1 tsp oregano
- 1 tsp salt
- ¾ tsp cayenne pepper
- 2 tbsp. olive oil
- 4 salmon filets, skin on
- 1 lemon, cut in wedges

Directions:
1. In a shallow dish, combine all the seasonings. Press the salmon filets, flesh side down, into the seasonings to coat well.
2. Set to sear on medium heat and add the oil. Place

the salmon, skin side up, in the pot and cook until blackened, about 3 minutes.

3. Turn the filets over and cook another 5-7 minutes or until they reach desired doneness. Serve immediately with lemon wedges.

Nutrition Info:
• Calories 313,Total Fat 18g,Total Carbs 3g,Protein 34g,Sodium 368mg.

Coconut Shrimp With Pineapple Rice

Servings:4
Cooking Time: 45 Minutes

Ingredients:
• 2 tablespoons canola oil
• 1 can diced pineapple
• 1 yellow onion, diced
• 1 cup long-grain white rice
• 1½ cups chicken stock
• ½ cup freshly squeezed lime juice
• ¾ cup all-purpose flour
• 1 tablespoon kosher salt
• ½ teaspoon freshly ground black pepper
• 2 large eggs
• ½ cup coconut flakes
• ½ cup plain panko bread crumbs
• 10 ounces, deveined shrimp, tails removed
• Cooking spray

Directions:
1. Select SEAR/SAUTÉ and set temperature to HI. Select START/STOP to begin. Let preheat for 5 minutes.
2. Add the oil and heat for 1 minute. Add the pineapple and onion. Cook, stirring frequently, for about 8 minutes, or until the onion is translucent.
3. Add the rice, chicken stock, and lime juice. Assemble pressure lid, making sure the pressure release valve is in the SEAL position.
4. Select PRESSURE and set to HI. Set time to 2 minutes. Select START/STOP to begin.
5. When pressure cooking is complete, allow press to naturally release for 10 minutes. After 10 minutes, quick release remaining pressure by turning the pressure release valve to the VENT position. Carefully remove lid when unit has finished releasing pressure.
6. Transfer the rice mixture to a bowl and cover to keep warm. Clean the cooking pot and return to the unit.
7. Create a batter station with three medium bowls.

In the first bowl, mix together the flour, salt and pepper. In the second bowl, whisk the eggs. In the third bowl, combine the coconut flakes and bread crumbs. Dip each shrimp into the flour mixture. Next dip it in the egg. Finally, coat in the coconut mixture, shaking off excess as needed. Once all the shrimp are battered, spray them with cooking spray.
8. Place Cook & Crisp Basket into pot. Place the shrimp in basket and close crisping lid.
9. Select AIR CRISP, set temperature to 390°F, and set time to 10 minutes. Select START/STOP to begin.
10. After 5 minutes, open lid, then lift basket and shake the shrimp. Lower basket back into the pot and close the lid to continue cooking until the shrimp reach your desired crispiness.
11. When cooking is complete, serve the shrimp on top of the rice.

Nutrition Info:
• Calories: 601,Total Fat: 15g,Sodium: 784mg,Carbohydrates: 88g,Protein: 28g.

Pistachio Crusted Mahi Mahi

Servings: 6
Cooking Time: 20 Minutes

Ingredients:
• Nonstick cooking spray
• 6 fresh Mahi Mahi filets
• 2 tbsp. fresh lemon juice
• ½ tsp nutmeg
• ¼ tsp pepper
• ¼ tsp salt
• ½ cup pistachio nuts, chopped
• 2 tbsp. butter, melted

Directions:
1. Place the rack in the cooking pot. Lightly spray a small baking sheet with cooking spray.
2. Place the fish on the prepared pan. Season with lemon juice and spices. Top with pistachios and drizzle melted butter over the tops.
3. Place the pan on the rack and add the tender-crisp lid. Set to bake on 350°F. Cook fish 15-20 minutes or until it flakes easily with a fork. Serve immediately.

Nutrition Info:
• Calories 464,Total Fat 14g,Total Carbs 3g,Protein 77g,Sodium 405mg.

Tuna Patties

Servings: 2
Cooking Time: 50 Min

Ingredients:
- 5 oz. of canned tuna /150g
- 1 small onion; diced
- 2 eggs
- ¼ cup flour /32.5g
- ½ cup milk /125ml
- 1 tsp lime juice /5ml
- 1 tsp paprika /5g
- 1 tsp chili powder, optional /5g
- ½ tsp salt /2.5g

Directions:
1. Place all Ingredients in a bowl, and mix to combine. Make two large patties, or a few smaller ones, out of the mixture. Place them on a lined sheet and refrigerate for 30 minutes.
2. Close the crisping lid and cook the patties for about 6 minutes on each side on Roast mode at 350 °F or 177°C.

Flounder Veggie Soup

Servings: 10
Cooking Time: 20 Minutes

Ingredients:
- 2 cups water, divided
- 14 oz. chicken broth, low sodium
- 2 lbs. potatoes, peeled & cubed
- 1 onion, chopped
- 2 stalks celery, chopped
- 1 carrot, chopped
- 1 bay leaf
- 2 12 oz. cans evaporated milk, fat free
- 4 tbsp. butter
- 1 lb. flounder filets, cut in 1/2-inch pieces
- ½ tsp thyme
- ¼ tsp salt
- ¼ tsp pepper

Directions:
1. Add 1 ½ cups water, broth, potatoes, onion, celery, carrot, and the bay leaf to the cooking pot. Stir to mix.
2. Add the lid and set to pressure cooker on high. Set the timer for 8 minutes. When the timer goes off, use quick release to remove the lid.
3. Set cooker to sauté on med-low. Stir in milk, butter, fish, thyme, salt and pepper and bring to a boil.

4. In a small bowl, whisk together remaining water and cornstarch until smooth. Add to the soup and cook, stirring, until thickened. Discard the bay leaf and serve.

Nutrition Info:
- Calories 213, Total Fat 6g, Total Carbs 25g, Protein 14g, Sodium 649mg.

Oyster Stew

Servings: 4
Cooking Time: 12 Min

Ingredients:
- 3 jars shucked oysters in liqueur /300g
- 3 Shallots, minced
- 3 cloves garlic, minced
- 2 cups chopped celery /260g
- 2 cups bone broth /500ml
- 2 cups heavy cream /500ml
- 3 tbsp olive oil /45ml
- 3 tbsp chopped parsley /45g
- Salt and white pepper to taste

Directions:
1. Add oil, garlic, shallot, and celery. Stir-fry them for 2 minutes on Sear/Sauté mode, and add the heavy cream, broth, and oysters. Stir once or twice.
2. Close the lid, secure the pressure valve, and select Steam mode on High pressure for 3 minutes. Press Start/Stop. Once the timer has stopped, do a quick pressure release, and open the lid.
3. Season with salt and white pepper. Close the crisping lid and cook for 5 minutes on Broil mode. Stir and dish the oyster stew into serving bowls. Garnish with parsley and top with some croutons.

Tangy Catfish & Mushrooms

Servings: 4
Cooking Time: 10 Minutes

Ingredients:
- 2 tbsp. olive oil
- 4 catfish fillets
- 1/8 tsp salt
- ¼ tsp pepper
- 1 tbsp. fresh lemon juice
- ¼ lb. mushrooms, sliced
- 1 onion, chopped
- ¼ cup fresh parsley, chopped

Directions:

1. Add the oil to the cooking pot and set to sauté on medium heat.

2. Sprinkle the fish with salt and pepper and add to the pot. Drizzle lemon juice over the top.

3. Add the remaining ingredients and cook 3-4 minutes. Turn fish over and cook another 3-4 minutes or until it flakes with a fork and mushrooms are tender.

4. Transfer fish to serving plates and top with mushrooms. Serve immediately.

Nutrition Info:
• Calories 187, Total Fat 10g, Total Carbs 4g, Protein 20g, Sodium 131mg.

Succotash With Basil Crusted Fish

Servings: 4
Cooking Time: 65 Min

Ingredients:
• 4 firm white fish fillets; at least 1 inch thick
• 1 large tomato, seeded and chopped
• ½ small onion; chopped
• 1 bay leaf
• 1 garlic clove, minced
• 1 medium red chili, seeded and chopped
• ¼ cup mayonnaise /62.5ml
• 1 ½ cups breadcrumbs /195g
• ¼ cup chicken stock /62.5ml
• ¼ cup chopped fresh basil /32.5g
• 1 cup frozen corn /130g
• 1 cup frozen mixed beans /130g
• 1 cup butternut squash; cubed /130g
• 1 tbsp olive oil /15ml
• 1 tbsp Dijon-style mustard /15g
• ¼ tsp cayenne pepper /1.25g
• ½ tsp Worcestershire sauce /2.5ml
• 1 tsp salt; divided /5g
• Cooking spray

Directions:
1. Press Sear/Sauté and adjust to Medium. Press Start to preheat the pot. Heat the oil and sauté the onion, garlic, and red chili pepper in the oil for 4 minutes or until the vegetables are soft.

2. Stir in the corn, squash, mixed beans, bay leaf, cayenne, chicken stock, Worcestershire sauce, and ½ tsp or 5g salt. Seal the pressure lid, choose Pressure; adjust the pressure to High and the cook time to 5 minutes. Press Start.

3. Season the fish fillets with the remaining salt. In a small bowl, mix the mayonnaise and mustard. Pour the breadcrumbs and basil into another bowl.

4. Use a brush to spread the mayonnaise mixture on all sides of the fish and dredge each piece in the basil breadcrumbs to be properly coated.

5. Once the succotash is ready, perform a quick pressure release and carefully open the pressure lid. Stir in the tomato and remove the bay leaf.

6. Set the reversible rack in the upper position of the pot, line with aluminum foil, and carefully lay the fish in the rack. Oil the top of the fish with cooking spray.

7. Close the crisping lid and Choose Bake/Roast; adjust the temperature to 375°F or 191°C and the cook time to 8 minutes. Press Start.

8. After 4 minutes, open the lid. Use tongs to turn them over and oil the other side with cooking spray. Close the lid and continue cooking. Serve the fillets with the succotash.

Sweet & Spicy Shrimp Bowls

Servings: 8
Cooking Time: 5 Minutes

Ingredients:
• ½ cup green onions, chopped
• 1 jalapeno pepper, seeded & chopped
• 1 tsp red chili flakes
• 8 oz. crushed pineapple, drained
• 2 tbsp. honey
• 1 lime, zested & juiced
• 1 tbsp. olive oil
• 2 lbs. large shrimp, peeled & deveined
• ¼ tsp salt
• 2 cups brown rice, cooked

Directions:
1. In a small bowl, combine green onions, jalapeno, chili flakes, pineapple, honey, lime juice, and zest and mix well.

2. Add the oil to the cooking pot and set to saute on medium heat.

3. Sprinkle the shrimp with salt and cook, 3-5 minutes or until they turn pink.

4. Add the shrimp to the pineapple mixture and stir to coat.

5. Spoon rice into bowls and top with shrimp mixture. Serve immediately.

Nutrition Info:
• Calories 188, Total Fat 3g, Total Carbs 23g, Protein 17g, Sodium 644mg.

Fish Broccoli Stew

Servings: 4
Cooking Time: 20 Minutes

Ingredients:
- 1-pound white fish fillets, chopped
- 1 cup broccoli, chopped
- 3 cups fish stock
- 1 onion, diced
- 2 cups celery stalks, chopped
- 1 cup heavy cream
- 1 bay leaf
- 1 and 1/2 cups cauliflower, diced
- 1 carrot, sliced
- 2 tablespoons butter
- 1/4 teaspoon garlic powder
- 1/2 teaspoon salt
- 1/4 teaspoon black pepper

Directions:
1. Select "Sauté" mode on your Ninja Foodi.
2. Add butter, and let it melt.
3. Stir in onion and carrots, cook for 3 minutes.
4. Stir in remaining ingredients.
5. Close the Ninja Foodi's lid.
6. Cook for 4 minutes on High.
7. Release the pressure naturally over 10 minutes.
8. Remove the bay leave once cooked.
9. Serve and enjoy.

Nutrition Info:
- Calories: 298g; Fat: 18g; Carbohydrates: 6g; Protein: 24g

Caramelized Salmon

Servings: 4
Cooking Time: 10 Minutes

Ingredients:
- 1 tbsp. coconut oil, melted
- 1/3 cup Stevia brown sugar, packed
- 3 tbsp. fish sauce
- 1 ½ tbsp. soy sauce
- 1 tsp fresh ginger, peeled & grated
- 2 tsp lime zest, finely grated
- 1 tbsp. fresh lime juice
- ½ tsp pepper
- 4 salmon fillets
- 1 tbsp. green onions, sliced
- 1 tbsp. cilantro chopped

Directions:

1. Add the oil, brown sugar, fish sauce, soy sauce, ginger, zest, juice, and pepper to the cooking pot. Stir to mix.
2. Set to sauté on medium heat and bring mixture to a simmer, stirring frequently. Turn heat off.
3. Add the fish to the sauce making sure it is covered. Add the lid and set to pressure cooking on low. Set the timer for 1 minute.
4. When the timer goes off let the pressure release naturally for 5 minutes, the release it manually. Fish is done when it flakes with a fork.
5. Transfer fish to a serving dish with the caramelized side up.
6. Set cooker back to sauté on medium and cook sauce 3-4 minutes until it's thickened. Spoon over fish and garnish with chopped green onions and scallions. Serve.

Nutrition Info:
- Calories 316,Total Fat 18g,Total Carbs 5g,Protein 35g,Sodium 1514mg.

Panko Crusted Cod

Servings: 4
Cooking Time: 15 Minutes

Ingredients:
- 2 uncooked cod fillets
- 3 teaspoons kosher salt
- ¾ cup panko bread crumbs
- 2 tablespoons butter, melted
- 1/4 cup fresh parsley, minced
- 1 lemon. Zested and juiced

Directions:

1. Pre-heat your Ninja Foodi at 390 °F and place the Air Crisper basket inside.
2. Season cod and salt.
3. Take a suitable and stir in bread crumbs, parsley, lemon juice, zest, butter, and mix well.
4. Coat fillets with the bread crumbs mixture and place fillets in your Air Crisping basket.
5. Lock Air Crisping lid and cook on Air Crisp mode for 15 minutes at 360 °F.
6. Serve and enjoy.

Nutrition Info:
- Calories: 554; Fat: 24g; Carbohydrates: 5g; Protein: 37g

Crab Alfredo

Servings: 4
Cooking Time: 25 Minutes

Ingredients:
- ½ cup butter, unsalted
- ½ red bell pepper, seeded & chopped
- 2 tbsp. cream cheese, low fat
- 2 cups half and half
- ¾ cup parmesan cheese, reduced fat
- 1 tsp garlic powder
- 2 cups penne pasta, cooked & drained
- 6 oz. lump crab meat, cooked

Directions:
1. Add butter to the cooking pot and set to sauté on medium heat.
2. When butter has melted, add bell pepper and cook until it starts to soften, about 3-5 minutes.
3. Add the cream cheese and cook, stirring until it melts.
4. Stir in half and half and parmesan cheese, and garlic powder until smooth. Reduce heat to low and simmer 15 minutes.
5. Stir in cooked penne and crab meat and cook just until heated through. Serve immediately.

Nutrition Info:
- Calories 388, Total Fat 23g, Total Carbs 26g, Protein 19g, Sodium 613mg.

Almond Crusted Haddock

Servings: 4
Cooking Time: 30 Minutes

Ingredients:
- 1 tbsp. sugar
- ¾ tsp cinnamon
- ¼ tsp red pepper
- ½ tsp salt
- 1 ½ lbs. haddock filets
- 1 egg white, beaten
- 2 cups almonds, sliced
- 2 tbsp. butter
- ½ cup Amaretto liqueur

Directions:
1. In a small bowl, combine sugar, cinnamon, red pepper, and salt until combined. Use 1 teaspoon of the mixture to season the fish.
2. Spray the fryer basket with cooking spray and place it in the cooking pot.

3. In a shallow dish, beat the egg white.
4. In a separate shallow dish, place the almonds. Dip each filet in the egg white then coat with almonds. Place them in the fryer basket and spray them lightly with cooking spray.
5. Add the tender-crisp lid and set to air fry on 350°F. Cook the fish 5 minutes, then turn over and spray with cooking spray again. Cook another 2-3 minutes until golden brown. Transfer to serving plate and keep warm.
6. In a small saucepan over medium heat, melt the butter. Add the remaining sugar mixture and Amaretto to the pan. Reduce heat to low, and cook, stirring, 1-2 minutes until sauce has thickened. Pour over fish and serve immediately.

Nutrition Info:
- Calories 576, Total Fat 30g, Total Carbs 26g, Protein 38g, Sodium 715mg.

Crab Cake Casserole

Servings: 8
Cooking Time: 17 Minutes

Ingredients:
- 2 tablespoons canola oil
- 1 large onion, chopped
- 2 celery stalks, chopped
- 1 red bell pepper, chopped
- 1½ cups basmati rice, rinsed
- 2 cups chicken stock
- ¼ cup mayonnaise
- ¼ cup Dijon mustard
- 3 cans lump crab meat
- 1 cup shredded Cheddar cheese, divided
- 1 sleeve butter crackers, crumbled

Directions:
1. Select SEAR/SAUTÉ and set to HI. Select START/STOP to begin. Let preheat for 5 minutes.
2. Add the oil. Once hot, add the onion, celery, and bell pepper and stir. Cook for 5 minutes, stirring occasionally.
3. Stir in the rice and chicken stock. Assemble pressure lid, making sure the pressure release valve is in the SEAL position.
4. Select PRESSURE and set to HI. Set time to 2 minutes. Select START/STOP to begin.
5. When pressure cooking is complete, allow pressure to naturally release for 10 minutes. After 10 minutes, quick release any remaining pressure by moving the

pressure release valve to the VENT position. Carefully remove lid when unit has finished releasing pressure.

6. Stir in the mayonnaise, mustard, crab, and ½ cup of Cheddar cheese. Top evenly with the crackers, then top with remaining ½ cup of cheese. Close crisping lid.

7. Select BAKE/ROAST, set temperature to 350°F, and set time to 10 minutes. Select START/STOP to begin.

8. When cooking is complete, open lid and serve immediately.

Nutrition Info:

• Calories: 448,Total Fat: 25g,Sodium: 819mg,Carbohydrates: 46g,Protein: 22g.

Salmon With Creamy Grits

Servings: 4
Cooking Time: 100 Min

Ingredients:

• 4 salmon fillets, skin removed
• 1½ cups vegetable stock /375ml
• ¾ cup corn grits /98g
• 1½ cups coconut milk /375ml
• 3 tbsps Cajun /45g
• 1 tbsp packed brown sugar/15g
• 3 tbsps butter; divided /45g
• 2 tsp s salt /10g
• Cooking spray

Directions:

1. Pour the grits into a heatproof bowl. Add the coconut milk, stock, 1 tbsp or 15g of butter, and ½ tsp or 2.5g of salt. Stir and cover the bowl with foil. Pour the water into the inner pot. Put the reversible rack in the pot and place the bowl on top.

2. Seal the pressure lid, choose Pressure; adjust the pressure to High and the cook time to 15 minutes. Press Start to begin cooking.

3. In a bowl combine the Cajun, brown sugar, and remaining salt.

4. Oil the fillets on one side with cooking spray and place one or two at a time with sprayed-side down into the spice mixture. Oil the other sides and turn over to coat that side in the seasoning. Repeat the process with the remaining fillets.

5. Once the grits are ready, perform a natural pressure release for 10 minutes. Remove the rack and bowl from the pot.

6. Add the remaining butter to the grits and stir to combine well. Cover again with aluminum foil and re-

turn the bowl to the pot (without the rack).

7. Fix the rack in the upper position of the pot and put the salmon fillets on the rack.

8. Close the crisping lid and Choose Bake/Roast; adjust the temperature to 400°F and the cook time to 12 minutes. Press Start. After 6 minutes, open the lid and use tongs to turn the fillets over. Close the lid and continue cooking.

9. When the salmon is ready, take out the rack. Remove the bowl of grits and take off the foil. Stir and serve immediately with the salmon.

Italian Flounder

Servings: 4
Cooking Time: 70 Min

Ingredients:

• 4 flounder fillets
• 3 slices prosciutto; chopped
• 2 bags baby kale /180g
• ½ small red onion; chopped
• ½ cup whipping cream /125ml
• 1 cup panko breadcrumbs /130g
• 2 tbsps chopped fresh parsley /30g
• 3 tbsps unsalted butter, melted and divided /45g
• ¼ tsp fresh ground black pepper /1.25g
• ½ tsp salt; divided /2.5g

Directions:

1. On the Foodi, choose Sear/Sauté and adjust to Medium. Press Start to preheat the inner pot. Add the prosciutto and cook until crispy, about 6 minutes. Stir in the red onions and cook for about 2 minutes or until the onions start to soften. Sprinkle with half of the salt.

2. Fetch the kale into the pot and cook, stirring frequently until wilted and most of the liquid has evaporated, about 4-5 minutes. Mix in the whipping cream.

3. Lay the flounder fillets over the kale in a single layer. Brush 1 tbsp or 15ml of the melted butter over the fillets and sprinkle with the remaining salt and black pepper.

4. Close the crisping lid and choose Bake/Roast. Adjust the temperature to 300°F or 149°C and the cook time to 3 minutes. Press Start.

5. Combine the remaining butter, the parsley and breadcrumbs in a bowl.

6. When done cooking, open the crisping lid. Spoon the breadcrumbs mixture on the fillets.

7. Close the crisping lid and Choose Bake/Roast. Adjust the temperature to 400°F or 205°Cand the cook

time to 6 minutes. Press Start.

8. After about 4 minutes, open the lid and check the fish. The breadcrumbs should be golden brown and crisp. If not, close the lid and continue to cook for an additional two minutes.

Clam Fritters

Servings: 4
Cooking Time: 10 Minutes

Ingredients:
- Nonstick cooking spray
- 1 1/3 cups flour
- 2 tsp baking powder
- 1 tsp Old Bay seasoning
- ¼ tsp cayenne pepper
- ¼ tsp salt
- ¼ tsp pepper
- 13 oz. clams, chopped
- 3 tbsp. clam juice
- 1 tbsp. lemon juice
- 2 eggs
- 1 ½ tbsp. chives, chopped
- 2 tbsp. milk

Directions:
1. Spray the fryer basket with cooking spray and add it to the cooking pot.
2. In a large bowl, combine flour, baking powder, Old Bay, cayenne pepper, salt, and pepper, mix well.
3. In a medium bowl, combine clams, clam juice, lemon juice, eggs, chives, and milk, mix well. Add the liquid ingredients to the dry ingredients and mix until combined.
4. Drop by spoonful into the fryer basket, don't over crowd them. Add the tender-crisp lid and set to air fry on 400°F. Cook 8-10 minutes until golden brown, turning over halfway through cooking time.

Nutrition Info:
- Calories 276,Total Fat 4g,Total Carbs 37g,Protein 21g,Sodium 911mg.

Drunken Saffron Mussels

Servings:4
Cooking Time: 25 Minutes

Ingredients:
- 2 tablespoons vegetable oil
- 2 shallots, sliced
- 3 garlic cloves, minced
- 1 cup cherry tomatoes, halved
- 2 pounds fresh mussels, washed with cold water, strained, scrubbed, and debearded, as needed
- 2 cups white wine (chardonnay or sauvignon blanc)
- 2 cups heavy cream
- 1½ teaspoons cayenne pepper
- 1½ teaspoons freshly ground black pepper
- ½ teaspoon saffron threads
- 1 loaf sourdough bread, cut into slices, for serving

Directions:
1. Select SEAR/SAUTÉ and set the temperature to HI. Select START/STOP to begin and allow to preheat for 5 minutes.
2. Add oil to the pot and allow to heat for 1 minute. Add the shallots, garlic, and cherry tomatoes. Stir to ensure the ingredients are coated and sauté for 5 minutes.
3. Add the mussels, wine, heavy cream, cayenne, black pepper, and saffron threads to the pot.
4. Assemble the pressure lid, making sure the pressure release valve is in the VENT position.
5. Select STEAM and set the temperature to HI. Set the time to 20 minutes. Select START/STOP to begin.
6. When cooking is complete, carefully remove the lid.
7. Transfer the mussels and broth to bowls or eat straight from the pot. Discard any mussels that have not opened.
8. Serve with the bread and enjoy!

Nutrition Info:
- Calories: 882,Total Fat: 54g,Sodium: 769mg,Carbohydrates: 61g,Protein: 20g.

Desserts

Chocolate Peanut Butter And Jelly Puffs 94
Chocolate Brownie Cake .. 94
Vanilla Hot Lava Cake 95
Date Orange Cheesecake .. 95
Berry Vanilla Pudding 95
Cheese Babka 96
Vanilla Cheesecake 97
Almond Milk 97
Coconut Rice Pudding 97
Baked Apples With Pecan Stuffing 98
Raspberry Cheesecake 98
Caramel Walnut Brownies 98
Chocolate Mousse 99
Raspberry Cobbler 99
Citrus Steamed Pudding .. 100
Berry Apple Crisps 100

Red Velvet Cheesecake 100
Chocolate Bread Pudding With Caramel Sauce 101
Apple Cider 101
Pumpkin Crème Brulee ... 102
Classic Custard 102
Lime Muffins 102
Coconut Pear Delight 102
Blueberry Peach Crisp 103
Raspberry Lemon Cheesecake 103
Buttery Cranberry Cake ... 103
Coconut Cream Dessert Bars 104
Chocolate Rice Pudding .. 104
Mexican Chocolate Walnut Cake 104

Chocolate Peanut Butter And Jelly Puffs

Servings:4
Cooking Time: 15 Minutes

Ingredients:
- 1 tube prepared flaky biscuit dough
- 2 milk chocolate bars
- Cooking spray
- 16 teaspoons (about ⅓ cup) creamy peanut butter
- 1 cup confectioners' sugar
- 1 tablespoon whole milk
- ¼ cup raspberry jam

Directions:
1. Remove biscuits from tube. There is a natural width-wise separation in each biscuit. Gently peel each biscuit in half using this separation.
2. Break the chocolate into 16 small pieces.
3. Spray a baking sheet with cooking spray.
4. Using your hands, stretch a biscuit half until it is about 3-inches in diameter. Place a teaspoon of peanut butter in center of each biscuit half, then place piece of chocolate on top. Pull an edge of dough over the top of the chocolate and pinch together to seal. Continue pulling the dough over the top of the chocolate and pinching until the chocolate is completely covered. The dough is pliable, so gently form it into a ball with your hands. Place on the prepared baking sheet. Repeat this step with the remaining biscuit dough, peanut butter, and chocolate.
5. Place the baking sheet in the refrigerator for 5 minutes.
6. Place Cook & Crisp Basket in pot. Close crisping lid. Select AIR CRISP, set temperature to 360°F, and set time to 20 minutes. Select START/STOP to begin. Let preheat for 5 minutes.
7. Remove the biscuits from the refrigerator and spray the tops with cooking spray. Open lid and spray the basket with cooking spray. Place 5 biscuit balls in the basket. Close lid and cook for 5 minutes.
8. When cooking is complete, remove the biscuit balls from the basket. Repeat step 7 two more times with remaining biscuit balls.
9. Mix together the confectioners' sugar, milk, and jam in a small bowl to make a frosting.
10. When the cooked biscuit balls are cool enough to handle, dunk the top of each into the frosting. As frosting is beginning to set, garnish with any toppings desired, such as sprinkles, crushed toffee or candy, or mini marshmallows.

Nutrition Info:
- Calories: 663,Total Fat: 25g,Sodium: 1094mg,Carbohydrates: 101g,Protein: 14g.

Chocolate Brownie Cake

Servings: 6
Cooking Time: 35 Minutes.

Ingredients:
- ½ cup 70% dark chocolate chips
- ½ cup butter
- 3 eggs
- ¼ cup Erythritol
- 1 teaspoon vanilla extract

Directions:
1. In a microwave-safe bowl, stir in the chocolate chips and butter and microwave for about 1 minute, stirring after every 20 seconds.
2. Remove from the microwave and stir well.
3. Set a "Reversible Rack" in the pot of the Ninja Foodi.
4. Close the Ninja Foodi's lid with a crisping lid and select "Air Crisp".
5. Set its cooking temperature to 350 °F for 5 minutes.
6. Press the "Start/Stop" button to initiate preheating.
7. In a suitable, add the eggs, Erythritol and vanilla extract and blend until light and frothy.
8. Slowly add in the chocolate mixture and beat again until well combined.
9. Add the mixture into a lightly greased springform pan.
10. After preheating, Open the Ninja Foodi's lid.
11. Place the springform pan into the "Air Crisp Basket".
12. Close the Ninja Foodi's lid with a crisping lid and select "Air Crisp".
13. Set its cooking temperature to 350 °F for 35 minutes.

14. Press the "Start/Stop" button to initiate cooking.
15. Place the hot pan onto a wire rack to cool for about 10 minutes.
16. Flip the baked and cooled cake onto the wire rack to cool completely.
17. Cut into desired-sized slices and serve.

Nutrition Info:
• Calories: 302; Fats: 28.2g; Carbohydrates: 5.6g; Proteins: 5.6g

Vanilla Hot Lava Cake

Servings: 8
Cooking Time: 40 Min

Ingredients:
• 1 ½ cups chocolate chips /195g
• 1 ½ cups sugar /195g
• 1 cup butter /130g
• 1 cup water /250ml
• 5 eggs
• 7 tbsp flour/105g
• 4 tbsp milk /60ml
• 4 tsp vanilla extract /20ml
• Powdered sugar to garnish

Directions:
1. Grease the cake pan with cooking spray and set aside. Open the Foodi, fit the reversible rack at the bottom of it, and pour in the water. In a medium heatproof bowl, add the butter and chocolate and melt them in the microwave for about 2 minutes. Remove it from the microwave.
2. Add sugar and use a spatula to stir it well. Add the eggs, milk, and vanilla extract and stir again. Finally, add the flour and stir it until even and smooth.
3. Pour the batter into the greased cake pan and use the spatula to level it. Place the pan on the trivet in the pot, close the lid, secure the pressure valve, and select Pressure on High for 15 minutes. Press Start/Stop.
4. Once the timer has gone off, do a natural pressure release for 10 minutes, then a quick pressure release, and open the lid.
5. Remove the rack with the pan on it and place the pan on a flat surface. Put a plate over the pan and flip the cake over into the plate. Pour the powdered sugar in a fine sieve and sift it over the cake. Use a knife to cut the cake into 8 slices and serve immediately (while warm).

Date Orange Cheesecake

Servings: 8
Cooking Time: 20 Minutes

Ingredients:
• Butter flavored cooking spray
• 2 cups water
• 2 lbs. ricotta cheese
• 4 eggs
• ¼ cup sugar
• ¼ cup honey
• Juice & zest of ½ orange
• ¼ tsp vanilla
• 1 cup dates, soak in warm water 20 minutes, chop fine

Directions:
1. Place the trivet in the cooking pot and add 2 cups water. Spray a deep, 8-inch springform pan with cooking spray.
2. In a large bowl, beat ricotta cheese until smooth.
3. In a medium bowl, beat eggs and sugar 3 minutes. Fold into ricotta cheese.
4. In a small saucepan, heat honey over low heat, do not let it get hot, just warm.
5. Whisk in orange juice, zest, and vanilla until combined. Whisk into cheese mixture until combined.
6. Fold in dates and pour into prepared pan. Cover with foil.
7. Place the cheesecake in the cooking pot and secure the lid. Set to pressure cooking on high. Set the timer for 20 minutes.
8. When timer goes off use natural release to remove the lid. Transfer cheesecake to wire rack to cool completely. Cover and refrigerate at least 4 hours before serving.

Nutrition Info:
• Calories 343,Total Fat 17g,Total Carbs 32g,Protein 16g,Sodium 132mg.

Berry Vanilla Pudding

Servings: 4
Cooking Time: 35 Min + 6h For Refrigeration

Ingredients:
• 4 raspberries
• 4 blueberries
• 4 egg yolks
• ½ cup sugar /65g
• ½ cup milk /125ml

- 1 cup heavy cream /250ml
- 1 tsp vanilla extract /5ml
- 4 tbsp water + 1 ½ cups water /435ml

Directions:

1. Turn on your Foodi and select Sear/Sauté mode on Medium. Add four tbsps or 60ml for water and the sugar. Stir it constantly until it dissolves. Press Stop. Add milk, heavy cream, and vanilla. Stir it with a whisk until evenly combined.

2. Crack the eggs into a bowl and add a tbsp of the cream mixture. Whisk it and then very slowly add the remaining cream mixture while whisking. Fit the reversible rack at the bottom of the pot, and pour one and a half cup of water in it. Pour the mixture into four ramekins and place them on the rack.

3. Close the lid of the pot, secure the pressure valve, and select Pressure mode on High Pressure for 4 minutes. Press Start/Stop. Once the timer has gone off, do a quick pressure release, and open the lid.

4. With a napkin in hand, carefully remove the ramekins onto a flat surface. Let cool for about 15 minutes and then refrigerate them for 6 hours.

5. After 6 hours, remove them from the refrigerator and garnish them with the raspberries and blueberries. Enjoy immediately or refrigerate further until dessert time is ready.

Cheese Babka

Servings:8
Cooking Time: 30 Minutes

Ingredients:
- FOR THE DOUGH
- 1 packet dry active yeast
- ¼ cup water, warmed to 110°F
- ¼ cup, plus ¼ teaspoon granulated sugar, divided
- 2 cups all-purpose flour
- 2 large eggs, divided
- ½ teaspoon kosher salt
- 3 tablespoons unsalted butter, at room temperature
- ¼ cup milk
- FOR THE FILLING
- 8 ounces cream cheese
- ¼ cup granulated sugar
- 1 tablespoon sour cream
- 1 tablespoon all-purpose flour
- ½ teaspoon vanilla extract
- Zest of 1 lemon
- Cooking spray

- All-purpose flour, for dusting
- 3 tablespoons water
- TO MAKE THE DOUGH

Directions:

1. In a small bowl, combine the yeast, warm water, and ¼ teaspoon of sugar. Let sit 10 minutes until foamy.

2. Place the flour, yeast mixture, remaining ¼ cup of sugar, 1 egg, salt, butter, and milk into the bowl of stand mixer. Using the dough hook attachment, mix on medium-low speed until the dough is smooth and elastic, about 10 minutes.

3. TO MAKE THE FILLING

4. In a medium bowl, whisk together all the filling ingredients until smooth.

5. TO MAKE THE BABKA

6. Spray the cooking pot with the cooking spray. Place the dough in the pot. Cover the dough with plastic wrap and let it rise in a warm place until doubled in size, about 1 hour.

7. Spray the Ninja Multi-Purpose Pan or 8-inch baking pan with cooking spray.

8. Turn the dough out onto a floured work surface. Punch down the dough. Using a rolling pin, roll it out into a 10-by-12-inch rectangle. Spread the cheese filling evenly on top of the dough. From the longer edge of the dough, roll it up like a jelly roll.

9. Cut the roll evenly into 12 pieces. Place each piece cut-side up in the prepared pan. The rolls should be touching but with visible gaps in between.

10. Beat the remaining egg with 1 teaspoon of water. Gently brush the tops of the rolls with this egg wash.

11. Place the remaining 3 tablespoons of water in the pot. Place the pan on the Reversible Rack, making sure the rack is in the lower position. Then place the rack with pan in the pot.

12. Select SEAR/SAUTÉ and set to LO. Select START/STOP to begin.

13. After 5 minutes, select START/STOP to turn off the heat. Let the rolls rise for another 15 minutes in the warm pot.

14. Remove the rack and pan from the pot. Close crisping lid.

15. Select BAKE/ROAST, set temperature to 325°F, and set time to 30 minutes. Select START/STOP to begin. Let preheat for 5 minutes.

16. Place the rack with pan in the pot. Close lid and cook for 25 minutes.

17. Once cooking is complete, open lid and remove

rack and pan. Let the babka completely cool before serving.

Nutrition Info:
• Calories: 325,Total Fat: 16g,Sodium: 286mg,Carbohydrates: 38g,Protein: 7g.

Vanilla Cheesecake

Servings: 6
Cooking Time: 60 Min

Ingredients:
• 16 ounces cream cheese, at room temperature /480g
• 2 eggs
• ¼ cup sour cream /62.5ml
• 1½ cups finely crushed graham crackers /195g
• 1 cup water /250ml
• ½ cup brown sugar /65g
• 2 tbsps sugar /30g
• 1 tbsp all-purpose flour /15g
• 4 tbsps unsalted butter, melted /60ml
• 1½ tsp s vanilla extract /7.5ml
• ½ tsp salt /2.5ml
• Cooking spray

Directions:
1. Grease a spring form pan with cooking spray, then line the pan with parchment paper, grease with cooking spray again, and line with aluminium foil. This is to ensure that there are no air gaps in the pan. In a medium mixing bowl, mix the graham cracker crumbs, sugar, and butter. Spoon the mixture into the pan and press firmly into with a spoon.
2. In a deep bowl and with a hand mixer, beat the beat the cream cheese and brown sugar until well-mixed. Whisk in the sour cream to be smooth and stir in the flour, vanilla, and salt.
3. Crack the eggs in and beat but not to be overly smooth. Pour the mixture into the pan over the crumbs. Next, pour the water into the pot. Put the spring form pan on the reversible rack and put the rack in the lower positon of the pot.
4. Seal the pressure lid, choose Pressure, set to High, and set the time to 35 minutes. Choose Start/Stop to begin. Once done baking, perform a natural pressure release for 10 minutes, then a quick pressure release to let out any remaining pressure. Carefully open the lid.
5. Remove the pan from the rack and allow the cheesecake to cool for 1 hour. Cover the cheesecake with foil and chill in the refrigerator for 4 hours.

Almond Milk

Servings: 4
Cooking Time: 20 Min

Ingredients:
• 1 cup raw almonds; soaked overnight, rinsed and peeled /130g
• 2 dried apricots; chopped
• 1 cup cold water /250ml
• 4 cups water /1000ml
• 1 vanilla bean
• 2 tbsp honey /30ml

Directions:
1. In the pot, mix a cup of cold water with almonds and apricots. Seal the pressure lid, choose Pressure, set to High, and set the timer to 1 minute.
2. When ready, release the pressure quickly. Open the lid. The almonds should be soft and plump, and the water should be brown and murky. Use a strainer to drain almonds; rinse with cold water for 1 minute.
3. To a high-speed blender, add the rinsed almonds, vanilla bean, honey, and 4 cups or 1000ml water. Blend for 2 minutes until well combined and frothy. Line a cheesecloth to the strainer.
4. Place the strainer over a bowl and strain the milk. Use a wooden spoon to press milk through the cheesecloth and get rid of solids. Place almond milk in an airtight container and refrigerate.

Coconut Rice Pudding

Servings:6
Cooking Time: 8 Minutes

Ingredients:
• ¾ cup arborio rice
• 1 can unsweetened full-fat coconut milk
• 1 cup milk
• 1 cup water
• ¾ cup granulated sugar
• ½ teaspoon vanilla extract

Directions:
1. Rinse the rice under cold running water in a fine-mesh strainer.
2. Place the rice, coconut milk, milk, water, sugar, and vanilla in the pot and stir. Assemble pressure lid, making sure the pressure release valve is in the SEAL position.
3. Select PRESSURE and set to HI. Set time to 8 minutes. Select START/STOP to begin.

4. When pressure cooking is complete, allow pressure to naturally release for 10 minutes. After 10 minutes, quick release remaining pressure by moving the pressure release valve to the VENT position. Carefully remove lid when unit has finished releasing pressure.

5. Press a layer of plastic wrap directly on top of the rice (it should be touching) to prevent a skin from forming on top of the pudding. Let pudding cool to room temperature, then refrigerate overnight to set.

Nutrition Info:
• Calories: 363,Total Fat: 18g,Sodium: 31mg,Carbohydrates: 50g,Protein: 5g.

Baked Apples With Pecan Stuffing

Servings: 4
Cooking Time: 45 Minutes

Ingredients:
• 4 Fuji apples
• ½ cup pecans, chopped
• ¼ cup Stevia
• 2 tbsp. coconut oil, melted
• 1 tbsp. molasses
• ½ tsp cinnamon
• ½ cup water

Directions:
1. Hollow out the apples by carefully removing the core and seeds. Place in the cooking pot.
2. In a medium bowl, combine nuts, Stevia, oil, molasses, and cinnamon, mix well. Spoon into the apples, stuffing them fully.
3. Pour the water around the apples. Add the tender-crisp lid and set to bake on 350 °F. Bake 40-45 minutes. Let cool slightly before serving.

Nutrition Info:
• Calories 329,Total Fat 17g,Total Carbs 49g,Protein 2g,Sodium 11mg.

Raspberry Cheesecake

Servings: 6
Cooking Time: 30 Min

Ingredients:
• 1 ½ cups Graham Cracker Crust /195g
• ¾ cup Sugar /98g
• 1 cup Raspberries /130g
• 1 ½ cups Water /375ml
• 3 cups Cream Cheese /390g
• 3 Eggs

• ½ stick Butter, melted
• 1 tbsp fresh Orange Juice /15ml
• 1 tsp Vanilla Paste /5g
• 1 tsp finely grated Orange Zest /5g

Directions:
1. Insert the reversible rack into the Foodi, and add 1 ½ cups or 375ml of water. Grease a spring form. Mix in graham cracker crust with sugar and butter, in a bowl. Press the mixture to form a crust at the bottom.
2. Blend the raspberries and cream cheese with an electric mixer. Crack in the eggs and keep mixing until well combined. Mix in the remaining ingredients, and give it a good stir.
3. Pour this mixture into the pan, and cover the pan with aluminium foil. Lay the spring form on the tray. Select Pressure and set the time to 20 minutes at High pressure. Press Start. Once the cooking is complete, do a quick pressure release. Refrigerate the cheesecake for at least 2 hours.

Caramel Walnut Brownies

Servings: 4
Cooking Time: 60 Min+ Cooling Time

Ingredients:
• 2 large eggs, at room temperature
• 8 ounces white chocolate /240g
• 1 cup sugar /130g
• ½ cup caramel sauce/125ml
• ½ cup toasted walnuts /65g
• ¾ cup all-purpose flour /98g
• 8 tbsps unsalted butter /120g
• 2 tsp s almond extract /10ml
• A pinch of salt
• Cooking spray

Directions:
1. Put the white chocolate and butter in a small bowl and pour 1 cup or 250ml of water into the inner pot. Place the reversible rack in the lower position of the pot and put the bowl on top.
2. Close the crisping lid. Choose Bake/Roast; adjust the temperature to 375°F or 191°Cand the cook time to 10 minutes to melt the white chocolate and butter. Press Start. Check after 5 minutes and stir. As soon as the chocolate has melted, remove the bowl from the pot.
3. Use a small spatula to transfer the chocolate mixture into a medium and stir in the almond extract, sugar, and salt. One after another, crack each egg into the

bowl and whisk after each addition. Mix in the flour until smooth, about 1 minute.

4. Grease a round cake pan with cooking spray or line the pan with parchment paper. Pour the batter into the prepared pan and place on the rack.

5. Close the crisping lid and Choose Bake/Roast; adjust the temperature to 250°F or 122°C and the cook time to 25 minutes. Press Start. Once the time is up, open the lid and check the brownies. The top should be just set. Blot out the butter that may pool to the top using a paper towel.

6. Close the crisping lid again and adjust the temperature to 300°F or 149°C and the cook time to 15 minutes. Press Start. Once the time is up, open the lid and check the brownies. A toothpick inserted into the center should come out with crumbs sticking to it but no raw batter.

7. Generously drizzle the caramel sauce on top of the brownies and scatter the walnuts on top. Close the crisping lid again and adjust the temperature to 325°F or 163°C and the cook time to 8 minutes; press Start.

8. When the nuts are brown and the caramel is bubbling, take out the brownies, and allow cooling for at least 30 minutes and cut into squares.

Chocolate Mousse

Servings: 12
Cooking Time: 25 Minutes

Ingredients:
• Nonstick cooking spray
• 8 oz. semisweet chocolate chips
• 8 eggs, separated
• 1 teaspoon vanilla
• ¼ cup + 2 tbsp. powdered› sugar

Directions:
1. Spray an 8-inch springform pan with cooking spray. Line the bottom with parchment paper.
2. Melt the chocolate in a microwave safe bowl in 30 second intervals.
3. Beat the egg yolks until thick and pale. Slowly beat in the melted chocolate until combined. Fold in the vanilla.
4. Beat the egg whites with ¼ cup of sugar until soft peaks form. Fold ¼ of the egg whites into the chocolate mixture just until combined. Gently fold in remaining egg whites. Pour into the prepared pan.
5. Place the rack in the cooking pot and place the mousse on it. Add the tender-crisp lid and set to bake

on 350°F. Bake 20-25 minutes until almost set, the mousse will still be a little jiggly in the middle.

6. Transfer mousse to a wire rack and let cool completely. Cover and refrigerate at least 4 hours. Dust with remaining sugar before serving.

Nutrition Info:
• Calories 154,Total Fat 8g,Total Carbs 15g,Protein 5g,Sodium 48mg.

Raspberry Cobbler

Servings: 8
Cooking Time: 2 Hours

Ingredients:
• 1 cup almond flour
• ¼ cup coconut flour
• ¾ cup Erythritol
• 1 teaspoon baking soda
• ¼ teaspoon ground cinnamon
• 1/8 teaspoon salt
• ¼ cup unsweetened coconut milk
• 2 tablespoons coconut oil
• 1 large egg, beaten lightly
• 4 cups fresh raspberries

Directions:
1. Grease the Ninja Foodi's insert.
2. In a large bowl, mix together flours, Erythritol, baking soda, cinnamon and salt.
3. In another bowl, stir in the coconut milk, coconut oil and egg and beat until well combined.
4. Add the prepared egg mixture into the flour mixture and mix until just combined.
5. In the pot of the prepared Ninja Foodi, add the mixture evenly and top with raspberries.
6. Close the Ninja Foodi's lid with a crisping lid and select "Slow Cooker".
7. Set on "Low" for 2 hours.
8. Press the "Start/Stop" button to initiate cooking.
9. Place the pan onto a wire rack to cool slightly.
10. Serve warm.

Nutrition Info:
• Calories: 164; Fats: 12.5g; Carbohydrates: 10.9g; Proteins: 4.7

Citrus Steamed Pudding

Servings: 8
Cooking Time: 1 Hour

Ingredients:
- Butter flavored cooking spray
- 3 ½ cups water, divided
- 3 tbsp. + 1 tsp butter, soft
- 1 cup sugar, divided
- 2 tsp orange zest, finely grated
- 1 tbsp. + 2 tsp lemon zest, finely grated
- 2 eggs
- ¼ cup milk
- ¼ cup + 1 tbsp. orange juice, unsweetened, divided
- 2 cups self-rising flour, sifted
- 1 orange, peel & pith removed, chopped
- 1 ½ tbsp. cornstarch

Directions:
1. Spray a 6-cup oven-safe bowl with cooking spray. Pour 2 cups water in the cooking pot and add the steamer rack.
2. In a large bowl, beat 3 tablespoons butter, ½ cup sugar, and 4 teaspoons orange and lemon zest until smooth.
3. Beat in eggs, one at a time, and beating well after each addition.
4. In a small bowl, stir together milk and ¼ cup orange juice.
5. Fold flour, orange pieces, and milk mixture into butter mixture, alternating between ingredients, begin and end with flour.
6. Pour into prepared bowl and tent with foil. Tie with kitchen string and place on the steamer rack. Add the lid and set to steam. Cook 1 hour or until the pudding passes the toothpick test. Transfer to wire rack.
7. Drain any remaining water from the cooking pot. Set cooker to saute on medium heat.
8. Add remaining sugar and cornstarch to the pot. Slowly pour in 1 ½ cups water, stirring constantly until combined. Cook 5 minutes, or until thickened.
9. Stir in tablespoon of lemon juice, tablespoon orange juice, tablespoon lemon zest, and teaspoon butter and cook until butter has melted and mixture is smooth.
10. To serve: invert pudding onto serving plate and drizzle sauce over the top. Slice and serve.

Nutrition Info:
- Calories 305,Total Fat 8g,Total Carbs 54g,Protein 5g,Sodium 68mg.

Berry Apple Crisps

Servings: 8
Cooking Time: 30 Minutes

Ingredients:
- Butter flavored cooking spray
- 2 cups apples, peeled & chopped
- 2 cups blueberries
- 1 tbsp. lemon zest
- 1 tbsp. lemon juice
- ¼ cup + 1/3 cup honey, divided
- 1 tsp cinnamon
- ¼ tsp nutmeg
- 2 tbsp. cornstarch
- 2 ½ cups oats, divided
- ¼ cup walnuts, chopped
- 2 tbsp. coconut oil, melted

Directions:
1. Place the rack in the cooking pot. Lightly spray 8 ramekins with cooking spray.
2. In a medium bowl, combine apples, berries, zest, lemon juice and ¼ cup honey.
3. In a small bowl, stir together spices and cornstarch and sprinkle over fruit, toss gently to combine. Spoon into ramekins.
4. Add 1 ½ cups oats to a food processor or blender and pulse until they reach the consistency of flour. Pour into a medium bowl.
5. Stir the remaining oats and nuts into the oat flour. Add oil and 1/3 cup honey and mix until crumbly. Sprinkle over the tops of the ramekins.
6. Place ramekins on the rack and add the tender-crisp lid. Set to bake on 375°F. Bake 25-30 minutes until top is golden brown and filling is bubbly. Let cool slightly before serving.

Nutrition Info:
- Calories 280,Total Fat 8g,Total Carbs 38g,Protein 5g,Sodium 167mg.

Red Velvet Cheesecake

Servings:8
Cooking Time: 25 Minutes

Ingredients:
- 2 cups Oreo cookie crumbs
- 3 tablespoons unsalted butter, melted
- 2 packages cream cheese, at room temperature
- ½ cup granulated sugar
- ½ cup buttermilk

- 2 tablespoons unsweetened cocoa powder
- 1 teaspoon vanilla extract
- 2 tablespoons red food coloring
- ½ teaspoon white vinegar
- 1 cup water

Directions:

1. In a small bowl, combine the cookie crumbs and butter. Press this mixture into the bottom of the Ninja Multi-Purpose Pan or 8-inch baking pan.

2. In a large bowl, use an electric hand mixer to combine the cream cheese, sugar, buttermilk, cocoa powder, vanilla, food coloring, and vinegar for 3 minutes. Pour this over the cookie crust. Cover the pan tightly with aluminum foil.

3. Place the water in the pot. Insert Reversible Rack into pot, making sure it is in the lower position. Place the covered multi-purpose pan onto the rack. Assemble pressure lid, making sure the pressure release valve is in the SEAL position.

4. Select PRESSURE on HI. Set time to 25 minutes. Press START/STOP to begin.

5. When pressure cooking is complete, allow pressure to naturally release for 15 minutes. After 15 minutes, quick release remaining pressure by moving the pressure release valve to the VENT position. Carefully remove lid when unit has finished releasing pressure.

6. Remove cheesecake from the pot. Refrigerate for 3 hours, or overnight if possible before serving.

Nutrition Info:

- Calories: 437,Total Fat: 31g,Sodium: 338mg,Carbohydrates: 36g,Protein: 7g.

Chocolate Bread Pudding With Caramel Sauce

Servings: 14
Cooking Time: 3 Hours

Ingredients:

- Butter flavored cooking spray
- 8 cups whole wheat bread, cubed
- 1 cup dark chocolate chips
- ¼ cup cocoa powder, unsweetened
- ½ cup + 1/3 cup Stevia
- 1 cup pecans, chopped, divided
- 1/8 tsp salt
- 2 eggs
- 4 egg whites
- 1 2/3 cup skim milk, divided
- 1 cup almond milk, unsweetened
- 3 tsp vanilla, divided
- 1 tbsp. cornstarch

Directions:

1. Spray cooking pot with cooking spray. Add the bread cubes.

2. In a medium bowl, combine chocolate chips, cocoa, ½ cup Stevia, ¾ cup nuts, and salt, mix well.

3. Whisk in eggs, egg whites, 1 cup milk, coconut milk, and 1 teaspoon vanilla until smooth. Pour over bread and stir to make sure all of the bread cubes are covered. Sprinkle remaining nuts over the top.

4. Add the lid and set to slow cooking on low. Cook 3 hours or until bread pudding passes the toothpick test.

5. In a medium saucepan, combine remaining Stevia and cornstarch. Stir in remaining milk and cook over med-low heat until sauce has thickened.

6. Remove from heat and stir in remaining 2 teaspoons vanilla. Drizzle over bread pudding and serve.

Nutrition Info:

- Calories 269,Total Fat 14g,Total Carbs 27g,Protein 8g,Sodium 60mg.

Apple Cider

Servings: 6
Cooking Time: 45 Min

Ingredients:

- 6 green apples, cored and chopped
- 1/4 cup orange juice /62.5ml
- 3 cups water /750ml
- 2 cinnamon sticks

Directions:

1. In a blender, add orange juice, apples, and water and blend until smooth; use a fine-mesh strainer to strain and press using a spoon. Get rid of the pulp. In the cooker, mix the strained apple puree, and cinnamon sticks.

2. Seal the pressure lid, choose Pressure, set to High, and set the timer to 10 minutes. Press Start. Release the pressure naturally for 15 minutes, then quick release the remaining pressure. Strain again and do away with the solids.

Pumpkin Crème Brulee

Servings: 4
Cooking Time: 3:00 Hours

Ingredients:
- 1 egg yolk
- 1 egg, lightly beaten
- ¾ cup heavy cream
- 4 tbsp. pumpkin puree
- 1 tsp vanilla
- 4 tbsp. sugar, divided
- ¾ tsp pumpkin pie spice

Directions:
1. In a medium bowl, whisk together egg yolk and beaten egg, mix well.
2. Whisk in cream, slowly until combined.
3. Stir in pumpkin and vanilla and mix until combined.
4. In a small bowl, stir together 2 tablespoons sugar and pie spice. Add to pumpkin mixture and stir to blend.
5. Fill 4 small ramekins with mixture and place in the cooking pot. Carefully pour water around the ramekins, it should reach halfway up the sides.
6. Add the lid and set to slow cooking on low. Cook 2-3 hours or until custard is set.
7. Sprinkle remaining 2 tablespoons over the top of the custards. Add the tender-crisp lid and set to broil on 450°F. Cook another 2-3 minutes or until sugar caramelizes, be careful not to let it burn. Transfer ramekins to wire rack to cool before serving.

Nutrition Info:
- Calories 334,Total Fat 21g,Total Carbs 30g,Protein 6g,Sodium 59mg.

Classic Custard

Servings: 4
Cooking Time: 30 Minutes

Ingredients:
- Nonstick cooking spray
- 4 eggs
- ½ cup half and half
- 2 cups almond milk, unsweetened
- 1/3 cup Stevia
- 1 tsp vanilla
- ¼ tsp cinnamon

Directions:
1. Spray four ramekins with cooking spray.

2. In a large bowl, whisk all the ingredients together until combined. Pour into prepared ramekins
3. Place the ramekins in the cooking pot and pour enough water around them it comes ½ inch up the sides of the ramekins.
4. Add the tender-crisp lid and set to bake on 350°F. Bake 30 minutes or until custard is set. Transfer to a wire rack and let cool before serving.

Nutrition Info:
- Calories 135,Total Fat 5g,Total Carbs 23g,Protein 11g,Sodium 164mg.

Lime Muffins

Servings: 6
Cooking Time: 30 Min

Ingredients:
- 2 eggs plus 1 yolk
- 1 cup yogurt /130g
- ¼ cup superfine sugar/32.5g
- Juice and zest of 2 limes
- 8 oz. cream cheese /240g
- 1 tsp vanilla extract /5ml

Directions:
1. With a spatula, gently combine the yogurt and cheese. In another bowl, beat together the rest of the ingredients.
2. Gently fold the lime with the cheese mixture. Divide the batter between 6 lined muffin tins. Close the crisping lid and cook in the Foodi for 10 minutes on Air Crisp mode at 330 °F or 166°C.

Coconut Pear Delight

Servings: 2
Cooking Time: 15 Min

Ingredients:
- 2 Large Pears, peeled and diced
- ¼ cup Shredded Coconut, unsweetened /32.5g
- ¼ cup Flour /32.5g
- 1 cup Coconut Milk /250ml

Directions:
1. Combine all ingredients in your Foodi. Seal the pressure lid, select Pressureand set the timer to 5 minutes at High pressure. Press Start. When ready, do a quick pressure release. Divide the mixture between two bowls.

Blueberry Peach Crisp

Servings: 8
Cooking Time: 40 Minutes

Ingredients:
- 1 cup blueberries
- 6 peaches, peeled, cored & cut in ½-inch pieces
- ½ cup + 3 tbsp. flour
- ¾ cups Stevia, divided
- ½ tsp cinnamon
- ¼ tsp salt, divided
- Zest & juice of 1 lemon
- 1 cup oats
- 1/3 cup coconut oil, melted

Directions:
1. Place the rack in the cooking pot.
2. In a large bowl, combine blueberries, peaches, 3 tablespoons flour, ¼ cup Stevia, cinnamon, and 1/8 teaspoon salt, toss to coat fruit. Stir in lemon zest and juice just until combined. Pour into an 8-inch baking dish.
3. In a medium bowl, combine oats, ½ cup Stevia, coconut oil, remaining flour and salt and mix with a fork until crumbly. Sprinkle over the top of the fruit.
4. Place the dish on the rack and add the tender-crisp lid. Set to bake on 350 °F. Bake 35-40 minutes until filling is bubbly and top is golden brown. Serve warm.

Nutrition Info:
- Calories 265, Total Fat 11g, Total Carbs 44g, Protein 6g, Sodium 74mg.

Raspberry Lemon Cheesecake

Servings: 8
Cooking Time: 30 Minutes

Ingredients:
- Butter flavored cooking spray
- 8 oz. cream cheese, fat free, soft
- 1/3 cup sugar
- ½ tsp lemon juice
- 1 tsp lemon zest
- ½ tsp vanilla
- ½ cup plain Greek yogurt
- 2 eggs, room temperature
- 2 tbsp. white whole wheat flour
- Fresh raspberries for garnish

Directions:
1. Spray an 8-inch baking dish with cooking spray.
2. In a large bowl, beat cream cheese, sugar, lemon juice, zest, and vanilla until smooth.
3. Add yogurt, eggs, and flour and mix well. Spoon into prepared pan.
4. Place pan in the cooking pot and add the tender-crisp lid. Set to bake on 350°F. Bake 25-30 minutes or until cheesecake passes the toothpick test.
5. Transfer to a wire rack to cool. Cover with plastic wrap and refrigerate 2-3 hours. Serve garnished with fresh raspberries.

Nutrition Info:
- Calories 93, Total Fat 6g, Total Carbs 14g, Protein 5g, Sodium 127mg.

Buttery Cranberry Cake

Servings: 8
Cooking Time: 40 Minutes

Ingredients:
- Butter flavored cooking spray
- 2 eggs
- 1 cup sugar
- 3/8 cup butter, softened
- ½ tsp vanilla
- 1 cup flour
- 6 oz. fresh cranberries

Directions:
1. Set cooker to bake on 350°F. Spray an 8-inch baking pan with cooking spray.
2. In a large bowl, beat eggs and sugar until light in color and slightly thickened, about 5-7 minutes.
3. Add butter and vanilla and continue beating another 2 minutes.
4. Stir in flour just until combined. Gently fold in cranberries.
5. Spread batter in prepared pan and place in the cooking pot. Add the tender-crisp lid and bake 35-40 minutes or until the cake passes the toothpick test.
6. Remove from cooker and let cool in pan 10 minutes before transferring to a wire rack to cool completely.

Nutrition Info:
- Calories 259, Total Fat 10g, Total Carbs 40g, Protein 3g, Sodium 88mg.

Coconut Cream Dessert Bars

Servings: 10
Cooking Time: 2 Hour

Ingredients:
- Butter flavored cooking spray
- 1 cup heavy cream
- ¾ cup powdered Stevia
- 4 eggs
- ½ cup coconut milk, full fat
- ¼ cup butter, melted
- 1 cup coconut, unsweetened, grated
- 3 tbsp. coconut flour
- ½ tsp baking powder
- ½ tsp vanilla
- ½ tsp salt

Directions:
1. Spray cooking pot with cooking spray.
2. Place cream, Stevia, and coconut milk in a food processor or blender. Pulse until combined.
3. Add remaining ingredients and pulse until combined.
4. Pour mixture into cooking pot. Place two paper towels over the top. Add the lid and set to slow cooking on high. Cook 1-3 hours or until center is set.
5. Carefully remove lid so no moisture gets on the bars. Transfer cooking pot to a wire rack and let cool 30 minutes.
6. Refrigerate, uncovered at least 1 hour. Cut into 10 squares or bars and serve.

Nutrition Info:
- Calories 190,Total Fat 17g,Total Carbs 24g,Protein 4g,Sodium 236mg.

Chocolate Rice Pudding

Servings: 8
Cooking Time: 20 Minutes

Ingredients:
- 2/3 cup brown rice, cooked
- 2 cans coconut milk
- ½ cup Stevia
- ½ tsp cinnamon
- 1/8 tsp salt
- 1 tsp vanilla
- ½ cup dark chocolate chips

Directions:
1. Set cooker to sauté on medium. Add milk, Stevia, cinnamon, and salt and bring to a simmer, stirring frequently.
2. Stir in rice and reduce heat to low. Cook 15 minutes, stirring occasionally, until pudding has thickened.
3. Turn off cooker and stir in vanilla and chocolate chips until chocolate has melted. Serve warm or refrigerate at least one hour and serve it cold.

Nutrition Info:
- Calories 325,Total Fat 22g,Total Carbs 35g,Protein 3g,Sodium 62mg.

Mexican Chocolate Walnut Cake

Servings: 8
Cooking Time: 2 ½ Hours

Ingredients:
- Butter flavored cooking spray
- 1½ cups flour
- ½ cup cocoa powder, unsweetened
- 2 tsp baking powder
- 2 tsp ground cinnamon
- ¼ tsp cayenne pepper
- 1/8 tsp salt
- 1 cup sugar
- 3 eggs, beaten
- ¾ cup coconut oil melted
- 2 tsp vanilla
- 2 cups zucchini, grated
- ¾ cup walnuts, chopped, divided

Directions:
1. Spray the cooking pot with cooking spray and line the bottom with parchment paper.
2. In a medium bowl, combine dry ingredients and mix well.
3. In a large bowl, beat sugar and eggs until creamy.
4. Stir in oil, vanilla, zucchini, and ½ cup walnuts until combined. Fold in dry ingredients just until combined.
5. Pour batter into cooking pot and sprinkle remaining nuts over the top. Add the lid and set to slow cooking on high. Cook 2 ½ hours or until cake passes the toothpick test. Transfer cake to a wire rack to cool before serving.

Nutrition Info:
- Calories 452,Total Fat 28g,Total Carbs 48g,Protein 7g,Sodium 189mg.

Appendix A : Measurement Conversions

BASIC KITCHEN CONVERSIONS & EQUIVALENTS

DRY MEASUREMENTS CONVERSION CHART

3 TEASPOONS = 1 TABLESPOON = 1/16 CUP

6 TEASPOONS = 2 TABLESPOONS = 1/8 CUP

12 TEASPOONS = 4 TABLESPOONS = 1/4 CUP

24 TEASPOONS = 8 TABLESPOONS = 1/2 CUP

36 TEASPOONS = 12 TABLESPOONS = 3/4 CUP

48 TEASPOONS = 16 TABLESPOONS = 1 CUP

METRIC TO US COOKING CONVERSIONS

OVEN TEMPERATURES

120 °C = 250 °F

160 °C = 320 °F

180° C = 350 °F

205 °C = 400 °F

220 °C = 425 °F

LIQUID MEASUREMENTS CONVERSION CHART

8 FLUID OUNCES = 1 CUP = 1/2 PINT = 1/4 QUART

16 FLUID OUNCES = 2 CUPS = 1 PINT = 1/2 QUART

32 FLUID OUNCES = 4 CUPS = 2 PINTS = 1 QUART

 = 1/4 GALLON

128 FLUID OUNCES = 16 CUPS = 8 PINTS = 4 QUARTS = 1 GALLON

BAKING IN GRAMS

1 CUP FLOUR = 140 GRAMS

1 CUP SUGAR = 150 GRAMS

1 CUP POWDERED SUGAR = 160 GRAMS

1 CUP HEAVY CREAM = 235 GRAMS

VOLUME

1 MILLILITER = 1/5 TEASPOON

5 ML = 1 TEASPOON

15 ML = 1 TABLESPOON

240 ML = 1 CUP OR 8 FLUID OUNCES

1 LITER = 34 FL. OUNCES

WEIGHT

1 GRAM = .035 OUNCES

100 GRAMS = 3.5 OUNCES

500 GRAMS = 1.1 POUNDS

1 KILOGRAM = 35 OUNCES

US TO METRIC COOKING CONVERSIONS

1/5 TSP = 1 ML

1 TSP = 5 ML

1 TBSP = 15 ML

1 FL OUNCE = 30 ML

1 CUP = 237 ML

1 PINT (2 CUPS) = 473 ML

1 QUART (4 CUPS) = .95 LITER

1 GALLON (16 CUPS) = 3.8 LITERS

1 OZ = 28 GRAMS

1 POUND = 454 GRAMS

BUTTER

1 CUP BUTTER = 2 STICKS = 8 OUNCES = 230 GRAMS = 8 TABLESPOONS

WHAT DOES 1 CUP EQUAL

1 CUP = 8 FLUID OUNCES

1 CUP = 16 TABLESPOONS

1 CUP = 48 TEASPOONS

1 CUP = 1/2 PINT

1 CUP = 1/4 QUART

1 CUP = 1/16 GALLON

1 CUP = 240 ML

BAKING PAN CONVERSIONS

1 CUP ALL-PURPOSE FLOUR = 4.5 OZ

1 CUP ROLLED OATS = 3 OZ 1 LARGE EGG = 1.7 OZ

1 CUP BUTTER = 8 OZ 1 CUP MILK = 8 OZ

1 CUP HEAVY CREAM = 8.4 OZ

1 CUP GRANULATED SUGAR = 7.1 OZ

1 CUP PACKED BROWN SUGAR = 7.75 OZ

1 CUP VEGETABLE OIL = 7.7 OZ

1 CUP UNSIFTED POWDERED SUGAR = 4.4 OZ

BAKING PAN CONVERSIONS

9-INCH ROUND CAKE PAN = 12 CUPS

10-INCH TUBE PAN =16 CUPS

11-INCH BUNDT PAN = 12 CUPS

9-INCH SPRINGFORM PAN = 10 CUPS

9 X 5 INCH LOAF PAN = 8 CUPS

9-INCH SQUARE PAN = 8 CUPS

Appendix B : Recipes Index

A

Air Fried Scallops 81
Almond Crusted Haddock 90
Almond Milk 97
Aloo Gobi With Cilantro 50
Apple Cider 101
Apple Pecan Cookie Bars 22
Apple Walnut Quinoa 17
Apricot Bbq Duck Legs 64
Apricot Lemon Ham 74
Artichoke Bites 21
Asian Chicken Nuggets 24
Asian-style Meatballs 72

B

Baby Porcupine Meatballs 53
Bacon & Cranberry Stuffed Turkey Breast 57
Bacon Ranch Chicken Bake 65
Baked Apples With Pecan Stuffing 98
Baked Eggs & Kale 18
Baked Eggs In Spinach 19
Banana Custard Oatmeal 11
Beef And Broccoli Sauce 71
Beef Congee 70
Beef Jerky 71
Beef Mole 71
Beef Pho With Swiss Chard 79
Beef Stew With Beer 76
Beef, Barley & Mushroom Stew 70
Beets And Carrots 45
Bell Pepper Frittata 14
Berry Apple Crisps 100
Berry Vanilla Pudding 95
Blackened Salmon 85
Blueberry Peach Crisp 103
Braised Pork And Black Bean Stew 35
Breakfast Egg Pizza 14
Brisket Chili Verde 73
Brussels Sprouts Bacon Hash 17
Burrito Bowls 49
Butter Pork Chops 78
Butter-flower Medley 23
Buttered Turkey 66
Butternut Squash Cake Oatmeal 14
Butternut Squash, Apple, Bacon And Orzo Soup 41
Buttery Cranberry Cake 103

C

Caramel Walnut Brownies 98
Caramelized Salmon 89
Carrots Walnuts Salad 46
Cheese Babka 96
Cheesy Basil Stuffed Chicken 58
Cheesy Chicken & Mushrooms 65
Cheesy Corn Casserole 46
Cheesy Meat Omelet 12
Cheesy Onion Dip 31
Cheesy Shakshuka 10
Cheesy Tomato Bruschetta 25
Chicken And Quinoa Soup 59
Chicken Bites 21
Chicken Bruschetta 65
Chicken Chickpea Chili 64
Chicken Chili 36
Chicken Enchilada Soup 33
Chicken Noodle Soup 35
Chicken Pot Pie 63
Chicken Potpie Soup 37
Chicken Thighs With Cabbage 57
Chicken Tomatillo Stew 38
Chicken With Roasted Red Pepper Sauce 66
Chicken With Tomatoes And Capers 61
Chickpea, Spinach, And Sweet Potato Stew 36
Chipotle Raspberry Chicken 58
Chocolate Bread Pudding With Caramel Sauce 101
Chocolate Brownie Cake 94
Chocolate Chip And Banana Bread Bundt Cake 13
Chocolate Mousse 99
Chocolate Peanut Butter And Jelly Puffs 94
Chocolate Rice Pudding 104
Chorizo Mac And Cheese 53
Chorizo Omelet 15
Cinnamon Apple Bread 10
Cinnamon Roll Monkey Bread 13
Citrus Glazed Halibut 82
Citrus Steamed Pudding 100
Clam Fritters 92
Classic Custard 102
Coconut And Shrimp Bisque 42
Coconut Cream Dessert Bars 104
Coconut Pear Delight 102
Coconut Rice Pudding 97
Coconut Shrimp With Pineapple

Rice 86
Corned Beef 74
Crab Alfredo 90
Crab Cake Casserole 90
Crab Rangoon's 25
Cranberry Lemon Quinoa 16
Creamy Pumpkin Soup 41
Crème De La Broc 46
Crispy Cheesy Zucchini Bites 23
Crispy Chicken Skin 26
Crispy Delicata Squash 27
Crispy Kale Chips 52
Crispy Onion Rings 29
Crispy Roast Pork 75
Cuban Flank Steak 73
Cumin Baby Carrots 30

D

Date Orange Cheesecake 95
Deviled Eggs 10
Double Berry Dutch Baby 19
Drunken Saffron Mussels 92

E

Easy Clam Chowder 84
Eggplant & Penne Pot 50

F

Farfalle Tuna Casserole With Cheese 81
Fish Broccoli Stew 89
Fish Chowder And Biscuits 39
Flaxseeds Granola 15
Flounder Veggie Soup 87

G

Garlic-herb Chicken And Rice 62
Ginger Orange Chicken Tenders 60
Gingered Butternut Squash 22
Glazed Walnuts 28
Goulash (hungarian Beef Soup) 33
Greek Chicken 56
Green Bean Casserole 30
Green Minestrone 48
Green Squash Gruyere 54

H

Ham & Broccoli Frittata   11
Hearty Breakfast Muffins   9
Hearty Veggie Soup   51
Herb Roasted Drumsticks   59
Herb Roasted Mixed Nuts   23
Herbed Lamb Chops   76
Herby Fish Skewers   30
Holiday Honey Glazed Ham   77
Homemade Vanilla Yogurt   9
Honey Garlic Chicken And Okra   56
Honey Short Ribs With Rosemary Potatoes   72

I

Italian Baked Zucchini   49
Italian Flounder   91
Italian Sausage With Garlic Mash   45
Italian Sausage, Potato, And Kale Soup   39

J

Jamaican Jerk Chicken Stew   37

K

Kung Pao Shrimp   81

L

Lamb Tagine   69
Lasagna Soup   34
Layered Taco Casserole   69
Leeks And Carrots   48
Lemon Chicken   62
Lime Glazed Pork Tenderloin   74
Lime Muffins   102
Loaded Potato Soup   40

M

Mediterranean Cod   83
Mexican Chocolate Walnut Cake   104
Mexican Street Corn Queso Dip   25
Mini Crab Cakes   27
Mini Turkey Loaves   60
Mississippi Pot Roast With Potatoes   68
Moroccan Beef   79
Mushroom And Wild Rice Soup   37
Mushroom Poutine   44

O

Oyster Stew   87

P

Pancetta Hash With Baked Eggs   17
Paneer Cutlet   53
Panko Crusted Cod   89
Paprika Chicken   59
Parsley Mashed Cauliflower   48
Peaches & Brown Sugar Oatmeal   12
Pesto With Cheesy Bread   51
Pho Tom   40
Pineapple Appetizer Ribs   46
Pistachio Crusted Mahi Mahi   86
Pistachio Stuffed Mushrooms   27
Poached Egg Heirloom Tomato   16
Polynesian Pork Burger   75
Pork Asado   68
Potato Samosas   28
Prosciutto Egg Bake   18
Pumpkin Breakfast Bread   15
Pumpkin Crème Brulee   102

R

Raspberry Cheesecake   98
Raspberry Cobbler   99
Raspberry Lemon Cheesecake   103
Red Velvet Cheesecake   100
Roasted Tomato And Seafood Stew   34
Rosemary Lemon Chicken   58
Rosemary Sweet Potato Medallions   54
Rustic Veggie Tart   47

S

Salmon Croquettes   22
Salmon With Creamy Grits   91
Sausage & Egg Stuffed Peppers   11
Savory Custards With Ham And Cheese   12
Scalloped Potatoes   28
Seafood Gumbo   82
Seared Scallops In Asparagus Sauce   83
Shredded Buffalo Chicken   60
Shrimp And Sausage Paella   85
Simple Beef & Shallot Curry   73
Sour And Sweet Pork   77
Sour Cream & Cheese Chicken   62
South Of The Border Corn Dip   22
Southern-style Lettuce Wraps   75
Spanish Steamed Clams   83
Speedy Pork Picante   68
Speedy Pork Stir Fry   77
Spicy Black Bean Dip   29
Spinach Casserole   9
Spinach, Tomatoes, And Butternut Squash Stew   51
Steak And Minty Cheese   26
Steamed Sea Bass With Turnips   84

Stir Fried Cabbage   54
Stir Fried Scallops & Veggies   85
Strawberry Snack Bars   26
Stuffed Manicotti   53
Stuffed Whole Chicken   56
Succotash With Basil Crusted Fish   88
Sweet & Spicy Shrimp Bowls   88
Sweet Bread Pudding   18
Sweet Potato Fries   31
Sweet Potato Gratin   24

T

Taiwanese Chicken   59
Tamale Pie   76
Tangy Catfish & Mushrooms   87
Tangy Chicken & Rice   61
Tangy Jicama Chips   29
Tasty Acorn Squash   47
Tender Butter Beef   70
Tex-mex Chicken Tortilla Soup   42
Tilapia With Spicy Pesto   84
Tuna Patties   87
Turkey Breakfast Sausage   61
Turkey Casserole   57
Turkey Enchilada Casserole   63
Tuscan Chicken & Pasta   64

V

Vanilla Banana Bread   13
Vanilla Cheesecake   97
Vanilla Hot Lava Cake   95
Vegan Stuffed Peppers   48
Vegetarian Stir Fry   50
Veggie Lasagna   44

W

Walnut Orange Coffee Cake   16
Whole Roasted Broccoli And White Beans With Harissa, Tahini, And Lemon   52

Z

Zesty Brussels Sprouts With Raisins   31
Zucchini & Beef Lasagna   78
Zucchini Quinoa Stuffed Red Peppers   45

Printed in Great Britain
by Amazon

38946516R00064